Sea Flavor

Sea
Flavor

✧ ✧ ✧ ✧ ✧ ✧ ✧ ✧ ✧ ✧ ✧ ✧ ✧ ✧ ✧ ✧ ✧ ✧ ✧

by HAYDN S. PEARSON

Essay Index Reprint Series

BOOKS FOR LIBRARIES PRESS
FREEPORT, NEW YORK

LIBRARY OF CONGRESS CATALOG CARD NUMBER:

68-58809

Dedication

✿ ✿

To MY FRIENDS in the little fishing village of Lanesville on Cape Ann this book is dedicated.

I do not know when I first thought of *Sea Flavor*. Perhaps it has been in my mind for a long time. In the 1700's, Pearsons settled in Newburyport—then as now a salty town. There are still Pearsons in the town and the surrounding countryside.

Father Pearson, for many years a minister-farmer in the village of Hancock, New Hampshire, used to say, "I want to live within sight of the hills, but once in a while my eyes get hungry for a look at the ocean."

I went to the State University at Durham, New Hampshire, in 1922. Durham is located at the head of tidewater on Oyster River. Great Bay swings inland back of Portsmouth—one of the beautiful regions of the Northeast. For years I had been studying the flora and fauna of the inlands. This was a new opportunity.

On one memorable Sunday in the fall of 1922 I decided to take a day's hike in the area around Dover Point. That day I met "Old Dick." I presume I once knew his last name, but he will always be Old Dick to me. He lived in a two-room, weather-grayed shanty above high-tide level at the edge of a big marsh. There was a grove of pines behind his cottage and a little rectangular building that he used for a shop, woodshed, and winter storage for his dory, lobster pots, and buoys.

That fall day as I came along the edge of the marsh, Old Dick was sitting on the granite step at the door of his home. He pushed his glasses onto his forehead, looked up at me, and smiled. That was the beginning of three years of rich friendship. Old Dick was an individualist, but he was kind, gentle, and a philosopher. He had roamed the world in his younger days. He knew the oceans and seas and foreign water fronts. He had a little money to see him through his sunset time.

He died one winter's night three years later. But in the three years I came to know him well. I was twenty-one when I went to college—older than most of my classmates. Perhaps that helped build the bond between us. Perhaps I, too, felt what Old Dick used to call the pull of the sea. We went fishing and clamming together. We cooked meals in his spotlessly clean kitchen-living room. From fall to spring I made regular visits whenever I had a few hours to spare or when I felt the need to get away from books and typewriter.

Old Dick gave me my first "seeing" look at the ocean. Last year in Lanesville, a few miles north of Gloucester, I spent another inspiring period by the sea. It was fun to sit around the old lobster shacks and listen to the old-timers' stories. It was fascinating to see men pull the lobster pots and haul the trap nets. I watched the trawlers and tuna boats fishing in the bay and saw them head up the Annisquam River to Gloucester with their catches. There's something appealing about a little fishing village—a village rich in 300 years of tradition. Lanesville, there on the granite bluffs above the cove, is just one of many. But in the breezes that whip down from the north, in the tidal pools that are cradled in the granite rocks, in the smell of the mud at low tide, in the murmuring voice of the ocean as the waves break on pier, rock, and beach, and in the beautiful sunsets that I watched across Ipswich Bay, there was the true flavor of the sea.

To all of you who helped in the making of this book, I want to say "thank you." If Father Pearson were preaching a sermon on the flavor of life, I think he would say, "Live richly; live kindly. Sea flavor is important, but remember that even more important is the flavor of life."

You men who know the ocean and who go down to the sea for a living know both the flavor of life and the flavor of the sea. To you this book is dedicated.

HAYDN S. PEARSON

The author is grateful to the editors of the following papers for permission to use editorials, articles, and essays that have been previously published: the *Boston Globe*, the *Boston Herald*, the *Christian Science Monitor*, the *New York Times*, the *Providence Journal*, the *Portland Telegram*, the *Richmond Times-Dispatch*, the *Springfield Republican*, the *Washington Evening Star*, and the *Worcester Telegram*.

Contents

✿ ✿

Sea Flavor

Flavor of the Sea

✿ ✿

EACH YEAR multitudes of human beings go to the ocean and in its mysterious power find strength and solace for taut minds and weary bodies.

The moods of the sea run the gamut of emotions. In summer, when waves roll gently on white-sand beaches and talk in low voices as they break against granite promontories, the ocean seems calm and benign. The warmth of Summer's heart blesses land and water; the tides ebb and flow in rhythmic precision; sheltered coves and small fishing villages drowse through hot days and blue-black nights.

The spreading salt marshes rest quietly. Marsh hawks slowly circle the sky on motionless wings; great blue herons stand poised like chiseled statues in black-banked marsh creeks. Drumlins with tufts of scrubby oaks and bayberry thickets lift above the flatness like sleeping giant dinosaurs. The waves of tan-white dunes roll landward from the sea.

As the tides slant back again to the ocean, spotted sandpipers run on the wet sand. Herring gulls ride the air currents, stand gossiping on the rocks, or argue over their food. Quawks flap methodically from beach or trap-net buoys to their heronries in the red pines of a valley in the dunes. At the edge of the hazy horizon ships plow steadily along their lanes, and black smoke floats in long streamers behind them. Over the ocean and the land that stretches beside it is the peace of summer.

As autumn draws on, the mood of the ocean changes. The trees along the shore drop their leaves, the marshes are seared by frost, and the beach grasses on dune crests are brown silhouettes against the sky. There's a different tone to the song of the waves and a hungry power to their assaults on the land that foils their charging ranks. Long, winding windrows of grass and kelp form patterns on the beaches.

Standing on a beach at night in the full of October's moon, one can hear the spirit of fall. It is the time of the great migra-

3

tion. The terns, gulls, and geese are returning from their season on northern tundras. Sometimes one can see the dark flashes against the moon as the birds course southward. Strange cries come from their throats.

Autumn brings a new flavor—and a new beauty to the sea. But it has in its beauty a tinge of the ominous. Even on a glory day, when the whitecaps catch the glints of the sun and the hills that watch the water paint a carpet of gold and scarlet, the ocean's restless power is evident.

As autumn slides into winter, the sea's mood intensifies. No longer is there a sense of peace and quiet. Now comes the time of travail and testing of strength. The lobstermen pull up their pots for the last time of the year, and gray smoke spirals from the shanties by old piers as men repair equipment, make buoys, and knit new heads for their traps. Dories are pulled high on the land above the danger line. This is the period when sun and moon combine to throw highest tides against the shore.

Winter is the season when naked emotions are let loose. Periodically, great storms arouse the sea's strength. When a savage northeaster coincides with a high tide, all the awesome power of the ocean is flung into the battle. Waves throw themselves high into the air where they hit granite abutments or harbor piers. They rage in frustration as bulwarks thwart their onslaught. When the temperature is low, great storms give birth to ice cakes on marshes and beaches. The writhing sea builds up ramparts against itself. A severe storm in winter is a part of the spirit of the ocean in the time of cold—cruel, impersonal, and bringing desolation. There are days when winter leashes its power, and the sun shines from a cloudless sky. Such a day has a flavor that is distinctive. There's a peculiar brilliance to the light. Far up and down the coast line one can see objects in sharp detail. There's a greenish, steel-gray hue to the water, and the waves that slither in on the cold sands make a clear pattern of white lace as they spread on the gently sloping surface and then turn unhurriedly back toward the ocean. But one always has the feeling that the ocean is biding its time and gathering its power for another assault on the land.

4

It is in the depth of spring that many feel the flavor of the sea is at its best. When April's capriciousness has worn itself out and time edges into May, the ocean has a message of heartening cheer. There's life along the shore as the birds return. Sea rocket, beach peas, and beach grass take on color. The bayberries' big green blossoms lie close on the twiggy branches. The gulls circle and climb and dive. Men go out in their dories at dawn to see what the harvest is in their lobster pots, and trawlers pull their nets along the ocean floor.

Each day the climbing sun takes a course nearer the pole of the horizons. The marshes change their drab winter blankets for coverings of green, and spikes of thatch grass make winding paths along the banks of the creeks. Quartz crystals glint in the sands of the dunes. Bluebirds throw their hearts to the new season from apple trees behind the white houses of old fishing villages. The ocean has lost the sullen anger of winter. The gray of its waves has changed to blue and green. The miracle of new life is unfolding along the shore, and the sea matches its mood to the land that holds it in check.

The flavor of the sea is mysterious and profound. It has cruel power and soft gentleness. It has called to men for ten times 10,000 years. Anyone who has an open heart and a sensitive spirit can find in its flavor much that will add to the joy of life.

Little Fishing Villages

✿ ✿

ALONG THE COAST LINE one finds little fishing villages wherever nooks and coves, harbors and estuaries give protection from the ocean's power. Long before Columbus sailed his three little ships across the ocean, men had traversed the North Atlantic and had edged slowly down the coast, exploring the inlets and bays. When the white men came from the Old World and began to hew a nation out of a new continent, it was natural that they should make their first settlements in protected spots along the ocean's edge.

To anyone who is sensitive to the pageant of history there is something deeply appealing in the little fishing villages today. There are tradition and meaning in the old, weathered wharves with their worn, splintery planks and moss-covered oaken piles. Small, cluttered fishing shanties sit in the sun beside the coves. Lobster pots are piled around them, and colored buoys hang above the plain board doors. Dories and skiffs ride at anchor close to the old ladders that lead down from the piers.

Back from the harbors stretch the narrow streets of the little villages. Usually a white spire of an old church overlooks a little common. It's likely that there's an old granite watering trough and a cast-iron statue—the latter a memorial to the men who fought for their nation in the wars of yesteryear. The main street has its stores and a filling station where the blacksmith shop was once located. On the side streets, shaded by tall protecting elms and maples, are the old-fashioned houses built a century or more ago—homes of the men who went down to the sea in quest of a living.

The old fishing villages drowse through summer's heat and withstand the great storms of winter. There's nothing pretentious about them. They are a part of the history of a nation—a nation still growing toward its destined stature.

Clam Digging

❁ ❁

THE SHOREMAN does not claim to be a philosopher. He usually has definite opinions of contemporary goings on but is content to leave problems of world import to the cycle of conferences that now seem to be an integral part of the international scene. He believes, however, that affairs would be settled more quickly if all men had an opportunity to dig a few clams.

Of course, it is pleasant to excavate enough clams for a good chowder made New England style, but there are values in clam digging that transcend material gain. When a man rises at dawn on a spring day and goes down to the mud flats at low tide, he is in a world of quiet beauty. Silver-gray ponds of mist dot the marshes that stretch between sea and mainland; long ribbons of fog hang low over twisting creeks; slanting sunrays paint a shimmering trail across the gentle swells of the grayish-green ocean. The new day's loveliness is punctuated by the lonesome calls of homeward-flying herons and by the staccato trills of savanna sparrows in the patches of thatch grass. The black mud flats reach down to the ocean's edge. The area is crisscrossed by small gullies and dotted with miniature pools where sea water has been left behind. The heavy mud glistens with moisture as the sun climbs higher.

Slowly and pleasantly the clam digger works with an old stubby-handled clam hoe. Mounds of wet mud make miniature pyramids, heaps that will be leveled when the tide comes in. One by one the clams fill the bucket. From a practical point of view it is good to wend one's way homeward with a sufficiency; but, as many know, clam digging is more than discovering a bed of *Mya arenaria*. It is a chance for a man to get himself in tune with the peace and beauty that bless a quiet spring day by the ocean.

Ocean Fog

WHEN ATMOSPHERIC CONDITIONS are right, vapor condenses to fine particles of water. If this condensation occurs at a distance above the land or water, the result is called a cloud; if it happens close above the surface of the ocean or mainland, it is labeled fog. When high twelve of the year has passed and there's a hesitant interlude before autumn starts crawling down from the northern tundras, the ocean seems to delight in taking a deep breath and blowing a fog over the coast line. Technically, it's due to temperature changes, but anyone who loves the sea and its myriad moods accepts the different kinds of fogs as a part of the wonder and mystery of the wide waters.

On a moonlit evening there's something breath-takingly beautiful as a grayish-white blanket unrolls on the black, restless water and edges nearer and nearer to the shore. Faster and faster it seems to come. Suddenly the watcher on a quiet stretch of beach or on a jutting rocky headland senses the fog around him. Gone is the view of the ocean's edge. On noiseless feet the vapors crawl up the sand, spread over the rocks, and envelop the flat, sprawling marshes. All that's left of the ocean is the sound of gentle waves lapping on the sand or on the rocks.

In the midst of the gray murkiness there's a poignant loneliness. The lights of the village above the cove are blotted out; the draggers and seiners anchored in the harbor disappear; the unseen dories make little grating noises as they rub gently against old stone piers. Out in the ocean lanes ships of the night sound their foghorns and the distance-mellowed blasts roll across the water and echo back from the hills behind the shore. Over all is the cool, dim light of the moon. In the morning the sun's fingers reach out and gather in the fog net as fishermen go forth for the day's harvest.

Gull Talk

✿ ✿

HERRING GULLS are a familiar part of the scene around the harbors. They ride the air currents in graceful casualness. They are buoyant balls of white on the waves. They sit in symmetrical rows on the old fishhouses and weather-grayed shanties of lobstermen, cluster on the wet rocks of the harbor's mouth at low tide, and perch on the winch posts of trawlers tied to granite piers and splintered wharves. Gulls are an integral part of the sea's flavor along the coast.

Perhaps the gulls are most interesting when they have something to say to each other. Their voice inflections are almost human and, alas, they frequently show some of the less desirable human traits when conditions do not meet with their favor. When the trawlers are cleaning fish offshore, hundreds of the big birds follow in the wakes of the ships for the offal. They scream in greedy excitement and cry in anger and frustration. It's a babel of confusion based on selfishness. Many times two gulls get hold of the same piece of fish and fight with tenacious rancor. On the rocks and beaches at low tide there's a constant squabble and unashamed display of self-interest.

But there are times when the gulls are in better mood. They float leisurely in the air, uttering soft, plaintive calls; they light on perches with great outstretchings of wings and settle down to a few minutes' rest with peculiarly human little noises that remind one of a tired person sinking into a comfortable chair. They stand around on rocks and beach like groups of persons after a big meal, discussing in desultory fashion items of news and bits of gossip. The big white birds are nuisances sometimes, but they help keep the coast line and harbors clean. Their talk runs the gamut from friendly discussion to senseless quarreling. Yes, there's something strangely human about the conversation of gulls.

Beach Plums

✿ ✿

IT IS INTERESTING that Mr. Webster had room in his dictionary
for beach fleas but not for beach plums. Even his definition of
plum has a peculiar reaction on one who likes to study words.
Noah said, "The plum is a drupe, larger than a cherry and
with an oblong stone." That has a dubious connotation to anyone who is associated with the language of modern teen-agers.

Prunus maritima is a shrub of definite personality and many
likable traits. To be sure, *Prunus* likes the upper edges of sandy
beaches and the protected nooks of the dunes, but he's willing
to come inland a few miles where the soil is sandy if he can
get the salt breezes when northeasters battle the land. All along
the ocean and a few miles inland from Nova Scotia to Virginia
the beach plums add a welcome note to the vegetation.

Usually only a yard or so high, *Prunus* occasionally grows to
8 or 10 feet or more. The crooked, scraggly, brown-bark stems
remind one of the irregular pattern of the staghorn sumac. The
ovate leaves are sharply fine-toothed, gray-green above and a
lighter shade on the underside. In May the shrubs are covered
with clusters of white blossoms. *Prunus* seems to take his time
during June and July, but slowly the spherical fruits begin to
put on their ripening costumes. The dark green gives way to
a tannish brown; this, in turn, changes to a deeper brown, then
to that beautiful purple or magenta that means the fruit is ripe.

There are those who favor other fruits, but the shoreman
knows that beach-plum preserve or beach-plum jelly on fresh,
hot, homemade biscuits is something that gives him a lift. In
fact, two or three extra biscuits and a couple of glasses of cold,
creamy milk are just about equal to juicy deep-dish apple pie.
Naturally, a man wants both at proper times. But he's sure that
the beach plum has a definite place and is happy to see that
some nurseries are now advertising the shrub for home planting.

Nannyberry

✿ ✿

A PEWTER-GRAY DAY in January is a good time to observe the bark patterns of trees. When low stratus clouds make a veil between sun and earth, the soft, filtered light emphasizes the intricate details of the bark and makes an etching of the main limbs and small twigs. One of the most interesting shrub-trees is the nannyberry, often called the sheepberry or sweet viburnum, cousin of the high-bush cranberry. A good place to study the nannyberry is along the northeastern coast line where stone walls ramble down across fields and pastures to below the high-tide mark.

There is no tree or shrub more easily distinguished in winter. The long, slender, reddish-brown buds are different in shape from those of other tall-growing shrubs. Often they are curved sufficiently to remind one of a miniature sickle. The buds at the twigs' ends that will develop into blossoms are swollen at their bases into balls the size of small marbles. The nannyberry is common over a wide stretch of eastern North America and often joins with sumacs and gray birches to make a dense hedge along walls and fences.

It seems to make its best growth within sight of the ocean. Individual shrubs, with their sturdy, twisted stalks and tangled branches, reach a height of 25 feet or more. In May the ends of the branches are a mass of fragrant, creamy-white flowers clustered into flattened cymes, reminding one of the blooms of perennial phlox. In early autumn the limbs bend with the crop of purplish-black oblong fruits. When the season draws to a close, the symmetrically veined leaves change to a rich, flaming red. The nannyberry is just one of the native shrubs that adds its beauty to the countryside along the ocean's edge. Its gray bark cloak above gray stone walls matches the gray of the sea beneath the January sky.

H. Armstrong Roberts

Colors in the Waves

✿ ✿

THERE IS BEAUTY in the ever-moving waves of water that ruffle across Ocean's breast and find their fulfillment against land and rock, salt meadow and beach. As Earth wheels its circle around the sun, the colors in the waves change to meet the moods of the seasons. In the time of low twelve, when winter's harshness sandpapers the line between water and mainland, the predominant color is an ominous, cold steel gray. Autumn brings a deep blue flecked with creamy lace as whitecaps break on the crests of waves. The dominant shade of spring and summer is a rich blue-green. Often the sun's slanting rays reflect a softly blended tan-saffron hue from the breaking waves' irregular rims.

It is in the heart of spring, however, that the beauty of the colors stages its annual exhibition. Before the quietness of summer lays a calming hand on the ocean, there are days of pressing winds that hurry waves shoreward. As the sun strikes the waves a score of yards from shore, the ridges of water reflect shades of green shot with fingers of purple, blue, and violet. Sudden broad banners of white, gray, and cream blossom against the slanting green rollers, briefly reflect the light, and then blend again into the darker mass that gave them birth.

Loveliest of all is the scene along a rocky shore line on a sunlit day when the green waves meet land's jagged outposts and leap into the air. Then the green mass changes to turrets and spires of white foam. Every few seconds a new mass of water seems to crouch for a moment at the base of the rocks, gather its strength, and fling itself in broken fragments to the sun. The light's rays pierce the shattered waves, and jewel-like gleams of red and orange, gold and ruby twinkle for an instant of beauty and then fade away. The ever-changing colors in the waves are part of the appeal of the sea.

Sharptail

THE FLAVOR of the sea can be absorbed in many different types of littoral localities. But there is one spot that offers many flavorings blended into a mood that is difficult to discover elsewhere. At the mouth of a lonely marsh creek where the sloping, black mudbanks know the ocean's pulsing incoming and rhythmic withdrawing, one is close to the heart of Nature. Here where the ocean stretches before and the marsh lies beyond is the chosen home of a small bird known to few.

When repeated several times in succession his scientific name sounds as though he might be a large, stately bird. But *Ammospiza caudacuta caudacuta* is the sharp-tailed sparrow, a small shy fellow who likes the areas around the mouths of creeks that lead into bogs and marshes. It requires time and patience to get acquainted with *Ammospiza* in June and July when the greenish-white eggs speckled with brown are concealed in the marsh grass and both parents are feeding the young. The nest is made of bits of seaweed and marsh grasses, and the sharptails attach it to sturdy stalks, high enough above ground to escape the rise of the tides.

Much of the time the birds keep on the ground, running busily along in the edge of the grass, heads held low. Occasionally one will pause as if listening, then stretch upward until he appears twice his ordinary height. Sometimes the beauty of a summer day gets into *Ammospiza*'s heart and he will take a brief flight a few yards into the air and circle his home stamping ground. He tries hard to sing a song that matches the day's blue sky and the white tips of the ocean's blue bedspread, but the best he can do is a wheezy, thin series of high-pitched notes.

Sharptail's head is large for his body; he has burnt-orange side whiskers. But it's his tail that is of particular interest. His rounded rudder with sharp-pointed stiff feathers gives him his name and a bit of distinction.

16

The Sea Beach

✿ ✿

THERE IS an indefinable quality about a beach that brings a response from a man's heart. There are many kinds of beaches, but fundamentally they are all of similar origin. There's something of the unfathomable mystery of life surrounding one as he stands on moist, tide-packed sand and looks out over the ocean to a haze-blurred horizon on a quiet summer day. On a bitter, windy day of late autumn, when great froth-fringed waves surge up the beach and disintegrate into thin gray sheets edged with bubbly white lacing, one senses the irresistible power of the ocean's eternal unrest.

Twice in each twenty-four hours the tides wax and wane. Twice a day through the cycling centuries the sea gathers its strength and hurls its legions at the shore ramparts; and twice in the circle of light and darkness the wounded and defeated remnants of waves are called back into the sea. Each time the tide assaults the beaches, changes are made. Twice a year, at the full of the moon in spring and fall, the great tides rise, and, if, by chance, a northeast storm accompanies them, the beaches and shore line suffer grievous attack by overwhelming might. Then, if one stands on a lonely stretch of beach or takes his place on a craggy granite headland, he can feel the cold, impersonal cruelty of Nature.

The origin of the beaches is part of the story of the earth's evolution. The same principles apply to the long stretches of beautiful sand as apply to the little circular beaches that dot the shore line between rocky promontories and wooded peninsulas, which extend probing fingers into the salt water.

The exact time that the beaches along the Atlantic coast began their creation—a creation still in progress—can only be conjectured; but it probably started when the curtain was being pulled on the ice age. Their time of birth was an epochal scene of Gargantuan confusion. There was indescribable chaos as great rivers burst from beneath the retreating glaciers. Torrents of

17

water spewed forth. It was almost as if an explosion had occurred. The rushing waters tumbled boulders, rocks, and gravel far eastward over the flat plain that runs along the edge of the continent.

In the awesome turmoil began the birth of the sand stretches. The great underwater mills of the sea gods went to work. The currents washed the rocks and gravel back and forth, back and forth. Great rocks were cracked into small ones and eventually became gravel. The gravel was ground and reground. As time went on the gravel itself was broken down into fine pieces and became sand. Then the waves took the sand. In some places it was driven against the shore. All but the fine particles of quartz were washed back into the ocean. Century after century the process continued and at last the sandy stretches of beach came into being.

Beautiful are the beaches that are spotted along the battle line between ocean and land. From the far North to the extreme South they afford lovely little spots where a man can be alone for a while and ponder the deeper meanings of life.

Bayberries

✿ ✿

ALONG THE BARREN sandy stretches of Long Island and Cape Cod, and north and south of these areas, the bayberry thickets make islands of tangled arms above the line of high tide. The rolling resonance of its scientific name, *Myrica carolinensis*, seems a bit out of keeping with the low, tangled, thick-growing clumps where rabbits and white-footed mice find sanctuary in the midst of the dunes' shifting sands. Early winter is a good time to see the clusters of small wax-coated berries, which cling tightly to the rough-barked, stubby stems.

Before man learned to make glass and build frameworks around wicks in dishes of oil, settlers by the seacoast gathered the berries in late autumn, boiled them in water, skimmed off the wax that rose to the top, and made candles in tall cast-iron molds. Here and there along the shore are those who still make the light givers that exude a tangy, pleasant fragrance as they burn.

The bayberry thickets are part of the picture along the coast. They grow on the beaches beyond the patches of silver-gray sea rocket; they crowd on the slanting sides of dunes and circle tiny ponds in the hollows. At the edges of woods where red pine, gray birches, and poplars conceal white-tailed deer, the bayberries form wide ramparts of protection. When June sunshine rests on the ocean, the blossoms lie along the stems like big, green, rough-haired caterpillars. When the blossoms fall, the berries begin to show in clusters of eight to ten. Oddly, one never seems to see clusters of similar-sized berries; there are always two or three big ones, two or three medium-sized ones, and two or three very small ones. They remind one of bunches of miniature grapes. The long, slender, serrated leaves have small, round grayish spots that look like oyster shells. If one picks a leaf, crushes it, and holds it to his nostrils, he gets the spicy aroma.

The bayberry is just a humble shrub that helps hold the land together on the sandy stretches—a familiar part of the picture along the mainland's rim.

Cedric G. Chase

Old Roads to the Sea

* *

THREE CENTURIES and more ago men with dreams in their hearts came to the New World and built small settlements on hillsides above sheltered coves. As a new nation pushed down its roots and spread its branches, roads were made across upland fields, around the edges of salt marshes, and along the ridges that overlook the sea. At irregular intervals side roads were made—roads that led down to the ocean.

Long years ago men used these paths. With horses and carts they went to the beaches after storms to gather loads of seaweed to enrich garden plots. Sand was hauled to spread on muddy stretches of main roads. Oftentimes there was an expanse of woodland between the farm and the salt water. On fall and winter days men and boys cut red oak, gray birches, and jack pines for fireplaces and old-fashioned stoves.

Most of the roads are neglected now. Three tracks still show in the grasses and shrubs—the two outside lines where wheels crunched over the gravel and the center track where a plodding horse scuffed a shallow path. Tangled bayberries crowd close along the sides of the road; gray birches and stunted sumacs are repossessing the narrow strips that men once cut for their needs. Nature yields to man's insistence, but as soon as he relaxes his attention, she takes back that which was wrested from her.

Through the turning seasons the old roads drowse patiently. For a time in a nation's history they served a purpose. Soon the land will be as it was for thousands of years before the first white-winged boats sailed across the great waters.

Northward Flight

✿ ✿

WHEN THE YEAR has reached the fifth month, one can feel the urgency of the season on beaches, dunes, and marshes. The great heavenly bodies have wheeled into position, and the time of Earth's annual miracle is fulfilled. The first faint tinges of green creep into the uplifted leaves of the rockets; slender spikes push upward from the crowns of beach grass. The pudgy buds along the arms of bayberries begin to crack their stitchings.

Now the land and sea enter a new cycle. Spring has freed itself from Winter's rough passion. Life-giving warmth rests on the land along the ocean, and the gray-green waters roll gently beneath the climbing sun. This is the time of the northward flight. One can see it in the daylight hours. In small and large numbers, the terns, geese, ducks, and gannets drive through the sky. Against the blue expanse studded with shaggy flocks of clouds grazing leisurely along, the groups of swiftly winging birds remind one of flotillas of tiny ships.

Standing on a quiet beach at midnight in May, one can hear the northward flights. Above the gentle monotone of the waves breaking easily on the sloping sand, the high, thin calls of the birds drop faintly to human ears. Looking upward to the dark, star-dotted infinity of space, one will see shadowy bodies flash across the waxing moon. There is a part of life's inscrutable mystery in the poignant loneliness of the high trail. The haunting cries of birds in the night as they wing their way northward to breeding grounds in swamps and tundras give proof that the new season has arrived.

Jaunty Troubadour

✿ ✿

THE SCARLET PIMPERNEL is a jaunty little troubadour who paints a picture of beauty along the sea's edge. He's not a showy, blatant fellow; on the contrary, he's modest and retiring. But there's something hearteningly friendly about him as he brings his fresh colors to the crannies and nooks in the rocks above the high-tide mark.

It seems as though the dictionary were unusually terse in defining this flower. It merely says, "Any of a genus (*Anagallis*) of herbs of the primrose family, esp. the scarlet pimpernel (*A. arvensis*) whose scarlet, white or purplish flowers close at the approach of rainy or cloudy weather." There's not a word about the contrast between the soft green foliage of the tiny one-stemmed plants and the grays and browns of the weathered granite rocks. There's nothing about the poignant appeal of the small five-petaled blossom that holds its open face to the sunshine and closes when the last rosy fingers of the sun reach across the ocean and pull the curtains for night.

Few flowers have the dainty loveliness of the scarlet pimpernel. Somehow it reminds one of a miniature brooch. The petals are a soft salmon-red shade. The tiny pistils have pinhead balls of gold on their tips. The heart of the blossom is a small spot of deeper color—a blending of blues, purples, and violets. Around the edge of this heart is a narrow scarf of scarlet, tinged at the border with ocean blue. Only a humble little member of the primrose family, the scarlet pimpernel lives its quiet life, lending a refreshing touch of color to the rocks beside the ocean.

Philip Gendreau, New York

Shore-line Trees

❀ ❀

THERE IS SOMETHING poignantly appealing about shore-line trees. Twisted, stunted, and often grotesque in shape, they are part of the scenery along the strip that marks the battle line between ocean and land. Through the long years they have withstood the great storms that come with the equinoxes; they have been battered and whipped in winter gales.

Half a century and more ago a seed of willow, maple, or birch was deposited in a small pocket of soil by a wind. There were clouds and fogs and rains; the temperature was warm. It may be that a bit of soil crumbled from a side wall and covered the seed at just the correct depth. Days went by with Nature providing the necessary elements. The hard covering cracked; a tiny rootlet went downward; a slender green spear shot upward to meet the sun. A shore-line tree was born. Perhaps only one in thousands or in tens of thousands finds just the right conditions. To that one comes the miracle of life.

Through the circling seasons of heat and cold, storms and good weather the tiny shoot grew into a tree. It was lashed and pulled and buffeted. Year by year the roots grew thick and strong. The scraggly limbs began to make a pattern against the sky. Season by season the branches grew a bit longer until Nature's inexorable processes were halted and life left the old tree.

To one who delights in savoring the flavor of the sea the story is complete. Along the shore one can read it—the little trees just starting their gallant battle, the trees in full vigor, and the bare skeletons of those that stand silhouetted against sky, ocean, and granite headlands. The shore-line trees are an integral part of life along the ocean's edge.

Old Wharves

✿ ✿

UP AND DOWN the length of the coast one finds old wharves
where little fishing villages nestle above coves and harbors. For
wherever men of the sea have settled, they have built wharves
to make their work easier. Many of the old ones were con-
structed a century and more ago. Through the generations, as
each new nation in the Western world has grown to greatness,
the wharves have served their purpose.

Some of the old ones are granite edged, built up from a foundation below low tide with great blocks of stone. Among the rocks
and gravel the tiny blossoms of scarlet pimpernel lift their five-
petaled faces. Down at the water line are spreading patches of
rockweed with their cylindrical-shaped pods. They remind one
of thick brown quilts spread tightly over the granite blocks. The
stone slabs above high tide's reach are weathered and grayed
by the storms of the cycling seasons. Green-gray lichens make
intricate patterns on their rough surface.

A majority of the old wharves in little fishing villages are con-
structed of wood. The surface is made of gray, weather-splintered
planks. They are stained and splotched, and the ends are creviced
and gouged from a thousand storms. Some of the long oaken
piles that hold the wharves are black and grimy; others are
green with moss. The rising of the tides, the fog, and the crashing waves in storms have kept the wood well preserved—for if
wood is kept wet all the time, it has a long span of usefulness.
There's nothing pretentious about the ancient wharves; they're
rough and battered and worn. Through winter· storm and summer heat they serve man's purposes—memorials to those who
long ago made homes along the coast and went down to the
sea in quest of a living.

Pools among the Rocks

✿ ✿

JUST AT THE EDGE of high tide one finds pools of salt water, which twice in each lunar day are refilled by offerings of the waves that come climbing up the rockweed-carpeted granite. Some are tiny, shining spots that remind one of the bright tin pans in which Grandmother used to set the milk; others are a dozen yards or more across, depending on the way the last glacier tumbled the rocks before it receded.

The pools reflect the mood of the day. On a quiet, sunny day of summer or early fall, the water is mirror clear. Long strands of brilliant green moss lie motionless. Shorter-stemmed mosses line the sides and sections of the bottom, their shades of green and brownish bronze forming a beautiful pattern of color that blends with the grays and tans and smoky purples of surrounding rock. Tiny ivory-white barnacles grow on the granite sides of the pools, their circular tops like Lilliputian volcanoes.

On days when streaked nimbus clouds or heavy fog blanket the coast line, the pools are dark. Quiet though the water is, the mosses and the granite are deeper in shade, matching the weatherman's disposition. In heavy rain the drops make an appealing lace design. Each drop starts a circle of ripples; the ripples meet like embryo waves and dissolve in intricate patterns of bubbles and foam. When a northeaster blusters the earth and sea, the tidal pools are whipped back and forth and the wind throws water over surrounding rims.

There's nothing spectacular or unusual about them. The little pools are just a part of the interesting formation along the line between ocean and land. Nursed by their mother, the sea, they are miniature oceans where forms of marine life find sanctuary.

Jellyfish

✿ ✿

A JELLYFISH is one of the peculiar animals of the ocean. The dictionary says, "Any of various marine free-swimming coelenterates having a body of jellylike consistency; a medusa. Many have long tentacles with stinging hairs which often cause great annoyance to bathers." It helps to know that a coelenterate is any member of a phylum of invertebrate animals, including the corals, sea anemones, jellyfishes, and hydroids, and that medusa refers to a jellyfish, not to the mythological Medusa slain by Perseus, who gave her head to Athena.

Along the shore these colored, soaplike bubbles apparently drift aimlessly with the motion of the water. But the story of the jellyfish is one of the most fascinating tales of marine life. The hydroid, which looks like a plant of seaweed, is in reality an animal. A slender tube connects the branches and stems, the so-called "flowers" and the cup-shaped "fruits." The flowers, which resemble miniature dahlias or the seed cups of garden poppies, perform separate functions in connection with the life processes of the animal. One flower may take in microscopic bits of food; another produces a fruit that ripens and becomes a free-swimming jellyfish. As these fruits mature they break apart, as from a nest of close-fitting saucers. The saucers turn upside down and off they go with small tentacles trailing behind.

Then comes another strange part of the cycle. The swimming medusae, the jellyfish that we see on the shore after a storm, lay eggs that have the power of locomotion from tiny hairs or cilia. In due time many of the eggs attach themselves to rocks, sunken logs, or harbor piles. In accordance with Nature's mysterious dictates, the eggs do not grow into jellyfish. They develop into the hydroid plant, and the cycle of growth is repeated until at the plant's maturity the young saucerlike jellyfish are released into the ocean water.

Medusa is a strange and complicated creature—one of the myriad forms of life that adds interest to the sea.

28

Bumblebee Peep

❈ ❈

THE BUMBLEBEE PEEP has a string of pleasant everyday names and a peculiarly formidable Latin nomenclature. The semipalmated (half-webbed feet) sandpiper is known to ornithologists as *Ereunetes pussilus,* but his shore-line friends call him sandpeep, hawkeye, oxeye, black-legged peep, peeper, beach peep, or bumblebee peep. He can be distinguished from the least sandpiper by his larger size and by his legs, which are a shade of dark gray, while those of the least peepers are greenish yellow.

From 6 to 7 inches long and with a wingspread of a foot, the feathered bumblebees put on an intermittent aerial circus from the time they arrive along northern coasts in late April or May until they leave in September. Groups of the long-billed, mottled gray and brown birds run along the sands, following the waves in and out. Suddenly, as if at command, they rise into the air. Over the beach they fly, turning, twisting, wheeling, climbing, diving in perfect military formation. They may circle out over the water; they may head landward and course over the dunes. But they always stay in group formation, always seem to change direction at the same instant. Then they return for another feeding foray on the wet sands.

Sometimes one of the little fellows will put on an almost ludicrous show reminiscent of a barnyard hen's performance. On a hot summer day he will kick out his port leg and then slowly, comfortably stretch it full length as if limbering up his muscles. Then he will repeat the process for the starboard side. Occasionally flocks will be seen taking naps under the lee of the dunes, their bills concealed in their back feathers.

The semipalmated piper has one difficulty that gets him into periodic trouble. His mouth is small and round, all out of proportion to his long, strong bill. If he tries to swallow too large a piece of food, he gets into a laughable predicament. He braces his feet, shakes his head from side to side, and goes through a series of contortions. His actions are similar to those of the herring gull when he attempts to swallow too large a piece of fish before the other gulls snatch it from him.

The summertime notes of the bumblebee peeps are definitely nonmusical. They are harsh and rasping, sounds similar to the protesting squeaks of a saw being sharpened. But in the spring the male flies some 30 to 40 feet above the sand, throwing out bars of sweet, musical notes. The shaky, soft, appealing trill is similar to that of the goldfinch.

The semipalmated piper is only one of the everyday birds along the coast, but he adds life to the shelving slopes of sands.

Driftwood

✿ ✿

THROUGH THE CENTURIES the waves of the ocean have followed the mandates of moon and sun. Twice in each lunar day the waters surge in from the body of the sea and break on beach, marsh, or granite headland. Twice in the same time the waters are pulled back to the heart of the sea. And always the waves carry something with them; always, when the tide is high, they cast driftwood on the land.

Pathos, tragedy, and mystery are often implied in the driftwood that comes to shore. Much of it is explainable—trees, branches, and pieces of stump roots. Somewhere, perhaps long miles away, the power of the ocean has cut into the land and taken the soil and trees that once grew on it. Branches may break off, and logs and stumps may come to rest on beaches or rocks many miles distant. Never is the coast line in *status quo;* it is always building up or breaking away. But when planks and boards and pieces of equipment come to rest, one puzzles over the story behind them. Has there been a wreck off the coast? Were these bits once part of a ship on which men sailed the sea roads? Sometimes a whole section of a ship comes to a final resting place on the beach or in the dunes. Perhaps the fury of a great storm has moved the skeletal fragment from its grave on the sloping shelf of the ocean's floor. High above average tide the pegged timbers lie for a while, stark against the sky. Then the shifting sands begin to accumulate around them, and in time all that remains are a few markers that indicate a bit of man's handiwork has come to rest.

Along the coast men gather the driftwood and dry it for use in stoves and fireplaces. The salted material makes beautiful flames of red and scarlet, blue and steel gray. As a man watches the flames curl back and forth and leap into the chimney, he wonders at the story behind the light and heat. Driftwood often serves a purpose, but it is also a part of the unfathomable mystery of the sea.

31

Cedric G. Chase

Drumlins

✷ ✷

THE LINE between the sea and the land is always changing. Beaches have been made by the waves and then have been reclaimed by the sea. Broad-spreading salt marshes have been carved from the mainland and taken by dominion of the thatch grass, marsh hay, and blackjack grass. As tides have washed in, the grasses and their roots have salvaged the silt and the mud and have built up the area. In other places great storms have sent powerful rollers against soft-soiled marshes and have battered deep stretches of soil into submission for the water to carry away. Rocks have been rolled onto beaches and against granite headlands; century after century the granite walls and cliffs have been battered and their outlines worn into new patterns.

In this fluid, ever-changing area between the ocean and the land, one of the most interesting geologic formations is the drumlin. The word is from the Gaelic druim and means the ridge of a hill. Webster says, "An elongate or oval hill of glacial drift."

There is evidence that when the last glacier left the Northeast, there were rolling hills and a great sandy plateau high above the sea. Rivers ran through the rock-strewn area to the ocean, which was perhaps many miles to the east of its present line. Through the centuries animal and plant life and, eventually, man arrived. Gradually, in many places, the land was cut down; gradually the ocean claimed more area. Bays were carved out; estuaries were formed; salt marshes were built up as the ocean washed in silt and mud. In the broad marshes were left the tops of hills and ridges. These are the drumlins we see today—the "islands" in the marshes.

Many of the larger drumlins are almost bare stretches of sand, but the smaller ones, from a quarter acre to several acres in size, are places of quiet appeal to anyone who takes time to think of Nature's inexorable processes. Centuries ago these glacial hills were much larger. Here were the homes of Indians and the gardens where they raised corn, pumpkins, and beans. There were tepees and huts of wood and brick; campfires blazed in the darkness. From these now shrunken spots red men went down to the mud flats to dig clams and to tend their fish traps; from these hills war parties went forth, north, west, and south, to battle their enemies. In the seventeenth century, when the white men came across the ocean in their wonderful winged canoes, the red men took their arms and implements and retreated inland to the sanctuary of the virgin forests. But they left behind them evidences of their life on the drumlins—heaps of clam shells, arrowheads, stone axes, skin scrapers, bits of rough pottery, and bones of animals they killed for food.

Now the drumlins lie in the marshes, covered with brush and bushes, dotted with red oaks, sumacs, gray birches, and poplars. Birds build nests there, and snakes sun themselves in the open spaces. Hardhack and wild roses make patches of color. At the time of great tides, the salt water covers the surrounding marshes, and then the drumlins are truly islands. There's nothing spectacular about them; they stand quietly through the cycling seasons as Nature sends her alternating periods of cold and warmth. They are memorials to a yesteryear when the outlines of the continent were formed.

The Killdeer

❀ ❀

THERE IS a satisfying and fitting quality to the killdeer's scientific name, for it is in keeping with his general attitude toward life. *Oxyechus vociferous vociferous* is an extrovert of the first order. From the spring day he arrives along the northern coast until he leaves at season's end, his shrill, piercing cries sound over the marshes, shore line, and the upland area that borders the ocean. All summer long he is filled with buoyant exuberance.

Oxyechus is a friendly bird. Some of his family nest along the dry upper edges of the marshes, but many of them choose upland fields that overlook the ocean. The nest is carelessly woven of grasses. The four buff eggs are blotched with irregular markings of lavender, brown, and black. It is easy to identify this bird because of the two distinctive black bands across the lower neck and upper breast. The lower part of the back is a rich chestnut; when in flight much white shows in the wings. On the beach or in a freshly mown hayfield the meadow plover, as farmers call him, keeps bobbing his head up and down.

When the lady killdeer is surprised on her nest, she puts on an act that reminds one of a ruffed grouse's technique. She jumps in front of the intruder, drags her wings as if in distress, flounders about, shrieks loudly and piteously, and uses every artifice to induce a man to go after her. After he has followed her a score of yards, she miraculously recovers and soars away in strong flight. When the eggs hatch, the baby birds are funny little tykes that resemble the parents within a day.

The friendly killdeers are swift and graceful in the air or running along on their high, stilted legs. On a moonlit evening in midsummer they may be heard taking flight in the semi-darkness. "Killdee, killdee," they cry. They fit well into the environment along the shore.

35

Oysters

✧ ✧

OYSTERS ARE PECULIAR in some respects, but there are observers of contemporary goings on who gently suggest that *Homo sapiens* should proceed cautiously before offering comments on other species of life. Perhaps it is fortunate that oysters have uses other than in stews and casseroles. Scientists inform us that one oyster may lay 500 million eggs in a season and that if starfish, ghost shrimps, and ducks did not care for the raw bivalves, the ocean bed would soon be a mass of oyster shells.

Ostrea's life is not complicated. It gathers its food by opening and closing its hinged shells and drawing the sea water through its gills. It grows faster if it happens to start life below the low-tide line. If nearer to the shore, there are periods each day when it keeps its shell closed until the tide begins to come in.

Contrary to popular opinion, the beautiful pearls of milady's outfit are not from the genus of edible oysters. This other branch of the family secretes a solution manufactured from the carbonate of lime in ocean water. There's a pleasing ancient superstition to the effect that pearls were formed from drops of dew that had hardened in the air, were blown into the ocean, and then were swallowed by oysters. Webster's definition, though more prosaic, tells the facts: "A dense shelly concretion, lustrous and varying in color, formed as an abnormal growth within the shell of some mollusks, and used as a gem."

There are beautiful iridescent colors that glow from the insides of the shells. These rainbow hues result from the substance nacre, or mother-of-pearl, which the oysters use to line their homes. The soft blending beauty is caused by the microscopic furrows that break the rays of light and reflect them as individual colors. When one picks up an empty shell washed to the high-tide line by the rollers, he can see in the blended symphony of colors some of the beauty of the lace-topped waves.

Chondrus Crispus

✿ ✿

IRISH MOSS is just a humble member of the multitudinous sea-weed family. It clings tenaciously to rocks from the low-water mark to a depth of about 14 feet at ebb tide. There's beauty in the spreading patches of the dwarfed, thick-growing plant. On a calm summer day when the tide is out, the rocks appear caparisoned in a rich blanket of shimmering colors. There are shades of deep blue and dark green, overlays of purple, violet, and reddish bronze. As the moisture evaporates from the densely tufted carpet, some of the colors intensify; others fade to soft pastels, reminding one of a disappearing rainbow.

Chondrus responds to the mood of the great waters. When the sea is calm, the moss at shore's edge appears flat and broad. When the sea is roiled and showing its temper, it is curly and bunched. According to tradition, early in the 1800's Irishmen in Carragheen, near Waterford, Eire, discovered the valuable properties of the crinkly plant. For more than a century now, men and women, boys and girls have been harvesting this crop of the sea along the northeastern coast line of this country. When dried and processed, *Chondrus crispus* has valuable gelatinous qualities for making puddings, syrups, jellies, medicines, paints, cosmetics, and flavorings. Science is constantly devising new uses for it.

This seaweed has two growth periods—one in May and one in August. During these periods the moss gatherers can be seen along the shore line harvesting it with long rakes and drying it on the rocks in the hot summer sun. A handful of the bleached yellowish-gold moss softened with water will fill one's living room with the tangy fragrance of the ocean. Just a humble little plant that grows at the ocean's rim, *Chondrus crispus* serves man's needs in many ways and adds beauty to the line where water and land meet.

George French

A Humble Creature

IT IS TIME the modest, unobtrusive clam had a word said about its admirable psychological traits. It's a humble creature, to be sure, and lacks the zip and flair of the oyster, which always seems to have a good press. But the clam is an excellent example of the fundamental tenet of democracy. It has its peculiarities and idiosyncrasies, but in a democracy a person or animal should be allowed certain deviations from the norm as long as these individualities do not unduly conflict with the rights and privileges of peers.

Mya arenaria, the common thin-shelled bivalve mollusk, wouldn't take a prize for beauty. He has a wide rubbery foot that pulls him along on the mud, where he likes to make explorations when he comes up from below the surface. His long siphon neck is a very efficient tube with orifices. Through one of the holes water is taken in; through the other it is expelled. *Mya's* mouth is peculiarly placed inside his shell, near his foot, and his food is the plankton, the tiny sea animals, that come in with the water. The female lays her eggs with careless abandon in the water. When they hatch, the offspring swim about for a time and then bury themselves in the sand while they grow toward maturity.

Clams are interesting, but a man is chiefly concerned with their uses. There are some who like them steamed and dipped in butter; others prefer clam fritters and cream of clam soup. A few insist on scalloped clams; many hold out for fried clams. All are good, and the adherents of each school show commendable tenacity in argument. But for the genuine, best, most flavorful goodness of the bivalve mollusk, nothing quite equals a first-class clam chowder. Made with plenty of clams, rich creamy milk, plenty of tried-out fat pork, and enough onions to give that essential zip, it's a dish that warms a man's system and gives him ample nourishment until the next meal.

Beauty in the Dunes

✷ ✷

THE DUNES lie inland from the sea, beyond the line of average high-water level. To those who are insensitive to the moods of Nature they may be grimly desolate spots. They see only the waves of sand, the haunting loneliness, the brooding barrenness, and the stunted and dying trees overwhelmed by the shifting waves of inorganic particles. They see the sculptured ridges that the winds' fingers have carved on the face of a dune and the long, tangled roots of beach grass hanging from the tops of dunes, exposed to sun and storm. To them the dunes are places to be avoided, places that are both depressing and bleak.

But to one who responds to the flavor of the sea and to all the aspects of life along the shore line, there is beauty in the dunes. Many know the appeal of the great sand stretches in all seasons of the year, for the true nature lover recognizes their grandeur and attraction in the heart of winter as well as when the sun courses close to the pole of the horizon. They vary from season to season and from year to year. Part of their charm is their ever-changing pattern. After every wind and rain they are different. Like the waves of the ocean, these sand waves constantly change form.

There is life in the dunes. Clumps of beach grass grow on the sides and tops. Their roots go deep for water and their spike blooms seem like beautiful etchings. Sometimes the winds shift the sand and cover a patch of grass. If not buried too deeply, the tips grow up to the light. If the shift was great, the area is bare for a time until the seeds from other clumps are dropped and the miracle of life occurs.

Here and there solitary red pines and groups of gray birches fight their lonely battles. The sand surges back and forth around them. Anyone who watches individual trees will see the high and low times of struggle. Battered and assaulted at intervals, with periods of rest between, the gaunt, twisted trees carry on.

On the sides of the dunes away from the ocean there are

stretches of poverty grass, or *Hudsonia*. This is a wiry, heather-like, low-growing shrub. Its closely furled leaves hold moisture through long periods of drought. In June the tiny golden five-petaled flowers make carpets of yellow dots among the gray-green of the leaves. Sometimes sand is blown over these stretches, and all one sees are the bright little dots of color that seem to rest on the ground.

One of the fascinating spots in the dunes is a hollow at the bottom of surrounding sand crests. Here, collected water makes a little pond, and lovely salmon-pink marsh mallow lifts its beautiful blossoms, reminding one of big hollyhocks. This largest of all wild flowers chooses a good location, protected from the winds by the hillocks and certain of its water supply in the hollow.

These low spots—sometimes tiny pools, sometimes an extensive area—are the heart of dune life. The pines and birches find footholds in them. Around the edges and among the trees are the dense, tangled clumps of bayberries. Swamp grass grows thick and tall. The beautiful wild beach peas bloom here in spring; the marsh pinks hold aloft their fragile blossoms on slender stems. Occasionally one finds the beginning of a cranberry bog where long, wirelike stems support the little single-file leaves of purple-red color.

In the larger low-lying areas the white-tailed deer make their homes. Here and there among the dunes one who is observant will see their trails leading to patches of blackjack grass. In the long-needled red pines the herons build their bulky loose-stick nests, and all night long their nasal quawks come through the darkness.

The wind sweeps back and forth, up and down. It digs out circular pockets and semicircular cuts. When one stands on a crest and looks out over the sand waves and the green hollows and sees the ocean on one side and the mainland on the other, he knows it's one of Nature's battlegrounds. Season by season the picture changes; the winds build up and the winds tear down. But in the sheltered hollows life goes on. It is neither desolate nor tragic. It is a part of Nature.

White Cedar

✿ ✿

ALONG THE ATLANTIC COAST from southern Maine to northern Florida one can find the white cedar. This tree is often confused with arborvitae, which can be easily identified by its flattened, frondlike branches. The Indians called the arborvitae the "featherleaf tree." The white cedar can be distinguished by its small, globular, brownish-purple cones. They are usually less than ½ inch in diameter and have thick scales that open on the inside, with several little winged seeds under each scale. The leaves of *Chamaecyparis thyoides* are very small and scale-like, and in the middle of the back of many of these scales is a circular greenish-cream gland.

Too few tree lovers know the charm of this scraggly tree of the coastal area. It doesn't like the stretches close to the shore or the ridges of sand dunes where the soil is dry. But back a bit from the sea's domain, in the innumerable swamps that dot the coast line, the white cedar makes its home. Here its roots can be in water for many months of the year.

The branches are slender, and the foliage seems thin compared with its cousin, the red cedar. Oftentimes *Chamaecyparis* sends out several main stems from its root crown. In a grove in the heart of a swamp where many white cedars grow closely, the lowest branches are bare and brown. They're just plain trees of the swamps along the coast, but they serve man's purposes for posts and railway ties and fill the air with their clean, sharp fragrance, forming shady islands of beauty amidst the reedy hummocks and pools of black water.

Savanna Sparrow

✿ ✿

THOSE WHO LIKE the beaches, dunes, and drumlins in the marshes, are certain to get acquainted with the savanna sparrow, who considers himself the keeper of the land's edge. In July and August, when other small birds are quiet, *Passerculus sandwichensis savanna* takes it upon himself to let the world know that one bird likes the hot sultriness of midsummer. He perches on a spear of beach grass or on a clump of debris left by high tide and sends his strident trill through the hot sunshine.

Very early in April *Passerculus* returns from his winter sojourn in the southern states and announces his version of spring. He is partial to the marshes, and for days after his arrival he spends much of his time singing while his mate searches for a homesite. He is not a particularly handsome fellow in his brownish coat streaked with sepia and rust. However, he does have a streak of yellow over his eye that gives him a jaunty, rakish look, and his pinkish legs and feet add a note of distinction.

The nest is on the ground beneath a clump of weeds and is made of grasses, bits of moss, and a few hairs. Here the lady lays four or five bluish-white eggs copiously decorated with cinnamon-brown flecks and splotches. Both Mr. and Mrs. Sparrow spend much time on the ground, and Mr. frequently stops a moment from his food hunting, braces his feet, lifts his head, and tosses a stream of shrill trills into the air.

Passerculus sandwichensis savanna is a cumbersome name for such a happy, optimistic little fellow, but he doesn't let it discourage him. He is a welcome part of the scene along the coast.

Lee A. Ellis

Painting the Dory

THERE IS a strong bond between a man and his boat. It makes no difference whether his is a large ship or a small one; he feels an intangible but deep-rooted affection for the boat that carries him on the great waters.

Perhaps the most intimate feeling for small boats is found among the lobstermen who push along the shore line from dawn to dusk, pulling their livelihood from the sea. Those who do not have powerboats use the sharp-bowed, steep-sided dories. They stand as they row from one bobbing, colorful buoy to another. It's a familiar picture to watch them haul the traps, take the lobsters, and drop the pots overboard. The dory and the man are partners against the sea.

Along in March, after the new pots for the season are built and the buoys are repainted, the men give the boats their annual painting. On sloping shelves above small harbors, on rocky piers and old plank wharves, men with grizzled faces and farseeing eyes work quietly and unhurriedly on their overturned dories. Each man has his favorite color or color combination—white, blue, red, black, and green. Sometimes superstition governs the choice of colors. An old man may say with a smile, "I've used white and blue for forty years. I've made a living—such as it is. I can make out another spell on the same kind of living." In the mellowing days of March they draw the strokes with steady, skillful hands. When dory-painting time arrives along the coast, men know winter's grip is loosening.

Poverty Grass

❁ ❁

THE DUNES lie between the beaches and good soil or between the tide-washed sands and the flat, drumlin-dotted salt marshes. On the seaward side of the wind-patterned escarpments one finds the clumps of beach grass with their long, tough leaves and blossom spikes that resemble tall timothy hay. It's on the leeward side, toward the marshes and farmland, that poverty grass makes its heart-warming, valiant stand against the ever-shifting winds and sands.

The wiry, sturdy stems sometimes grow in single clumps. Occasionally large areas are covered by the mottled gray-green-brown miniature bushes. The short, stubby leaves are a soft gray color, almost as if they had been dusted with buckwheat flour. In early summer the tiny five-petaled blossoms are golden stars against the light brown sand. In the center of the blossom, at the base of the exquisitely proportioned petals, is a minute golden ball with the pinheaded yellow stamens growing around it.

Poverty grass, or *Hudsonia*, to call it by its scientific name, is the first flower to appear on the dunes. Back in the second battle line it grows 8 or 10 inches or more above the sand. Close to the high dunes, where the sands travel whenever a wind blows, it may on occasion be almost covered. Then only the tips and a few bright blossoms show. But the long, twisting, deep brown roots with the hairlike feeding rootlets go far down into the sand for water, and when the great storms come and pile the comminuted soil particles over their heathery tops, it's only a matter of time until the little buds on brittle stems come poking up to the sunlight. It's only a humble, unpretentious plant, but it stands guard faithfully on the battleground of the dunes.

Quawk

✿ ✿

THE BLACK-CROWNED NIGHT HERON is a familiar bird along the coast. He's called the quawk by fishermen and shoremen, but that hardly does him justice when one considers his resonant scientific nomenclature—*Nycticorax nycticorax naerious*. A bird with a name like that should have individuality and a few idiosyncrasies.

The quawk has both. His shape is peculiarly ungainly, reminding one of a two-thirds-grown Dominique pullet with an overlong neck and an oversized head. His soft gray and white plumage is a strikingly beautiful combination and matches well the light tan shades of the dunes where he spends much time. Heronries are always interesting spots, and when a few hundred pairs of the night herons choose a grove of red pines among the dunes, there is constant noise and activity. Several pairs often make their bulky loose-stick nests in one tree. When the young are half grown, the grove sounds like a barnyard full of scolding hens.

In the early summer *Nycticorax* is busy both day and night carrying fish to the always complaining young in the nests. Back and forth the herons fly. One wonders when they rest. They flock to the beaches at low tide; they congregate on the mud flats in the salt marshes; they light on the kegs at the corners of fish traps by the shore line. At night their weird nasal cries punctuate the darkness.

The black-crowned night heron isn't a friendly bird. He tends strictly to his own affairs; but his presence along the area between sea and land adds interest and variety to Nature's forms of life.

Sloops of the Air

❁ ❁

ANYONE WHO HAS VISITED a fishing village or a seaport knows the herring gulls. They're the common gulls with pearl-gray backs and black-tipped wings—the birds that remind one of human beings. They stand around in the mud and on the ledges of walls at low tide, arguing over the high cost of living and exchanging bits of news. They quarrel incessantly at feeding times; they complain vociferously of another's good luck. Even on a peaceful midsummer day when a flock is resting between feedings, one can often hear querulous, low-pitched conversation.

When the draggers are poking along offshore cleaning fish and tossing the discarded sections overboard, hundreds of the strong-winged birds make a cloud in the air. Their shrill, truculent screams carry far across the water as they fight for the offal. A half dozen beat the air hard as they chase one with a chunk of food in its mouth. In a large percentage of cases the chased bird eventually drops its prize, and one of the others swoops it up, sometimes before it reaches the water. Then the whole process is repeated; one of the previous hunters becomes the hunted.

There are other moods, however. *Larus argentatus smithsonianus* likes to ride the gentle swells along the coast line; he likes to sit on the quiet waters of harbors and coves. Oliver Wendell Holmes described this mood aptly when he wrote, "The gull, high floating like a sloop unladen." One can watch the birds for hours as they sit "high floating."

The gulls make a beautiful sight as they ride the air currents. When the wind is right they coast gracefully up and down; they make great circles—often with their broad, powerful wings almost motionless. If the air motion is determined by currents that bounce upward from sea walls or rocky headlands, they change wing positions, dip or raise their bodies, to adjust themselves to the circumstances. They like to keep poised on an

49

upcurrent of air. With their bodies and wing surfaces slightly inclined, the upstreaming wind drives them forward effortlessly.

After the sun has dropped behind the dunes and while the evening's streamers of red, gold, purple, and orange are fading toward pastel shades that gradually blend into blue-gray, the flight of the gulls to their night quarters begins. Some of the groups fly just above the water; others are perhaps 100 feet in the air. They flap slowly along with methodical, unhurried beats. Sometimes they fly in loose flocks; often they string along for an hour or more, as lone birds or in small groups. Occasionally there's a continuous, evening-long flight.

The herring gulls are protected by law because of the service they render. They are the scavengers who eat the fish offal of the harbors; they cleanse the shore after a storm has tossed fish and crustaceans onto the land. Here and there along the coast one hears complaints that their population is getting too large. They are flying inland and harming crops. But in the main the gulls serve man's needs well. Certainly the sea would be minus much of its flavor without them, whether they are quarreling and screaming, riding the water like sloops, coasting the air currents, following the fishing boats, or resting quietly on the roof peaks of old fishhouses and the piles of old plank piers.

Horseshoe Crabs

✿ ✿

To ONE who has a feeling for history and a realization that life has been evolving on this planet through aeons of time there is something particularly interesting about horseshoe crabs. For some 300 million years the crabs and their ancestors have made tracks on the sandy beaches that slope upward from salt water.

Each spring the horseshoe crabs come out of the sea by the millions and perhaps tens of millions to perform the ritual ordained by age-old instinct. From the cold-water beaches of Maine to the hot sands of the southern coast line the crabs lay their eggs. Usually the shell-armored tribolites come from the water after dark. On a calm, moonlit night in June they can be seen pushing slowly up the beach, leaving clearly etched double furrows in the moist sand. Near the average line of high tide the females begin their labors. Back and forth they go, scraping shallow depressions an inch or two in depth. Here are laid the hundreds of round green-tinted eggs. The males edge over the nests and deposit the milt. In four to eight weeks, depending on the temperature of water and air, the eggs hatch, and within a short time the infant crabs seek sanctuary along the sea's edge in protected pools and grassy estuaries. During the first year the crabs molt many times, pulling themselves from their chitinous shells and emerging in soft new shells that harden in a few weeks.

The horseshoe crabs represent the oldest form of life of which we know. There is nothing especially exciting about them; they are just simple organisms that live in and near the ocean. Children gather the empty shells; they watch the stolid, phlegmatic fellows work their way down to the water after a storm has carried them high on the beaches, little realizing perhaps that they are a link with the dawn of history.

Winston Pote: A. Devaney, Inc., New York

Low Tide

SINCE MEN of long ago first looked in wide-eyed awe at the majesty of the ocean, they have wondered about the flood and ebb of the tide. Songs have been sung and poems written in praise of high tide and the great surfs that lash the arms of earth and rock that reach out into the ocean. Little has been the praise and scant the appreciation of the low tide.

One doesn't care to say much about low-tide time in certain harbors where men have built marts of industry close to the sea's edge. But out along the lonely stretches where the salt marshes slope gradually from the mainland to the ocean and where the granite crags make rocky shelves from cliffs into the water, low tide has charm and appeal.

There's a clean, pungent odor from the mud flats of rivers, estuaries, and the creeks that curve into the marshes. There one can see the long slender ribbons of eelgrass swaying gently to and fro, hiding countless snails and forms of marine life. At the lower edge of the beaches the moist sand is a firmly packed mass of comminuted particles of quartz, the result of thousands of years of grinding by the ocean's surgings. When the waters are low, there are long lengths of golden-brown, ruffled-edged kelp left at high-water mark, and windrows of dried thatch grass stretch along the beach—grass that was taken out to sea and then cast back. On the rocks the sea moss dries its outer leaves in the sun, and the rockweed hangs, a limp, wet carpeting. It isn't as spectacular as when the waves reach high in assault against the ramparts that hold them in check, but for anyone who loves life along the coast the time of low tide is generous with its gifts.

Sea Pinks

✿ ✿

ANYONE WHO WALKS on the salt meadows in midsummer knows the friendly rosy faces of the sea pinks, or marsh pinks as they are commonly called. They are cheerful everyday flowers that neither try to hide among the grasses nor try to overtop them. *Sabbatia stellaris* pushes its slender green-yellow stem to the height of a foot and then opens single blossoms at the tips of its branches.

The thin, narrow, pale green leaves are spaced in pairs along the wiry stalk. Near the top of the stem the leaves are very small, reminding one of tiny spears. When crushed, these leaves give off a rich, spicy fragrance that has just a suggestion of cinnamon. Hours afterward the nostril-tickling aroma can still be detected. The pinks' small faces, perhaps ½ inch across, are divided into five petals. The stamens are a deep yellow-orange, and the heart of the blossom is an unusual shade of greenish-yellow, edged with an irregular fringe of ocher or scarlet.

The sea pinks are peculiarly cosmopolitan in their acceptance of home sites. Most of them, it is true, are found on the spreading marshes that drowse beneath the hot summer sun. But they can also be found on the lower fringes of upland fields that slope down to the salt meadows. Here and there among the granite rocks of jutting spits are small gardens of the sweet-smelling pinks. Beneath the locusts and sumacs that line moss-etched cliffs, the small flowers bend before the breezes.

On a peaceful summer day when a few marsh hawks are skimming the grass tops and others are coasting the air currents high in the sky, when white sails dot harbors and earth and sea seem drowsing in the fullness of the season, the bright faces of the sea pinks add beauty to the marshes and to the edge of the mainland.

Sand Dollars

✿ ✿

IN MANY WAYS it is to be deplored that a system of exchange values cannot be evolved that is on a different basis from what is now used as coin of the realm. There's something to be said for a barter method based on values such as the Indians used. Perhaps wampum making would be a bit too slow and tedious for this modern era, but something is needed that will stimulate lads to work for spending money. There are arguments for mowing lawns, cleaning out ashes, and keeping the wood box filled. But these lack flair and zest. If a boy could only use sand dollars as an exchange medium for fishing tackle, ice-cream cones, hard candy, and four-bladed jackknives, he would be more interested in working. Sand dollars are like sea urchins; they have five distinct parts to their shells. They are thin, and a lad could easily keep a few dozen in his pockets.

The purplish-gray circular animals are covered with hairlike spines, which they use as legs. One needs patience to study them at the edge of low tide, as they pull themselves along infinitely slowly. What would life be like with no sense of time's urgency? This humble marine animal cannot live long out of water. Uncounted numbers are cast up on the shores and rocks each year to die in the light and air. Yet such is Nature's mysterious balance of life that the tremendous number of eggs given off by the females keep the species in existence. They feed on little pieces of seaweed taken into the mouth where the five sections of the shell meet.

Each year children find the dried white-tan sand dollars along the shore. What is their purpose? Why the millions of them in the sea? Unnoticed are many of the small forms of life, but they are all part of the mystery and fascination of the ocean's edge.

George French

Old Fishhouses

UP AND DOWN the coast line numberless old fishhouses dot the landscape. They nestle in the coves and harbors of little fishing villages and stretch along splintery piers built on moss-covered, decades-old oak and maple piles. Rows of the small shanties rest peacefully beneath rocky sea walls or at the foot of sprawling granite arms that stretch out toward the open sea.

They are called by various names—fishhouses, fishermen's shanties, or lobstermen's cabins. But what's in a name? There's an appealing picturesqueness to the small, dilapidated buildings that cling close to the ocean they serve. Some of them lean at precarious angles, shored up by pieces of rock or stubs of four-by-fours. They are grayed and weather-beaten. They drowse through the sultry heat of the year's high twelve while summer folk invade the coastal villages and exclaim at their quaintness.

Most of the fishhouses have been patched and repaired a score of times in the past generations. Bits of roofing paper and strips of tin have been put on to cover leaks. Perhaps an old burlap bag or a discarded oilskin is stuffed in a broken window. There's a stub of a metal chimney protruding from the roof, anchored against wintry gales with several taut stretches of wire. Around the outside there's a clutter of gear and debris, the accumulation of decades—broken lobster pots, discarded buoys, kegs used for lobster bait, buckets and pails, cork floats, old pieces of rope and wire, and, as the country auction bills proclaim, "other articles too numerous to mention."

Often there's a narrow winding path to the plain board door. Many of the fish shanties have granite doorsteps. Sometimes these are worn smooth and hollowed a bit in the center, memorials to the men and boys who fought for a living from the sea and, God willing, came back to land again.

There's something pleasant and comfortable about the interior of the old fishhouses. The pattern is similar in most of them. Across one end, before the grime-stained, cobwebby window, is a battered, gouged, waist-high workbench. On the bench and the rough shelves built above it is a tangled conglomeration of tools, string, paint pots, paint brushes, nails, and pieces of wood.

At the other end, the windowless one, there's a stack of cypress lathes and small-dimension oak lumber for making new lobster pots piled from the floor to the ceiling. Making new pots is an essential part of a lobsterman's business, for when great storms blow up suddenly in late autumn or early winter, a man sometimes loses his whole string. On spikes from the splintery two-by-four uprights hangs a collection of miscellaneous items, reminding one of the hall closet under the stairs in many a home. There are coils of rope and wire, round rings to be knitted into lobster heads, old oilskins, bags, twine, and freshly tarred twine heads. There are discarded anchors and newly painted buoys in single colors or combinations of red, yellow, blue, and orange.

At one side are the small rusty stove and the battered buckets for holding coal. On a blustery winter day when a gale is howling from the north or northeast, it's warm and cozy in the fish shanties as a man builds lobster pots or repairs his gear against the opening of a new season in March.

The pungent smell in the old fishhouses is better than the good fragrance of a country blacksmith shop or the combined atmosphere of the harness room and the shop on a farm. It's a blended aroma of paints, wood, creosote, twine, dirt, dust, old clothes, lobster bait, fish, and that indescribable, nostril-filling smell that hovers over an old harbor—that smell of moist mud, wet wood, seaweed, and sea moss that gives a bracing, heady tang to the air.

Here and there, artists, writers, and visitors have bought old fishhouses and have made them into summer homes. But many still fulfill their original purpose. From them in the fog-shrouded dawn men go forth to tend their lobster pots or to set their trap nets. To them they return when the day's work on the ocean is done before going to their homes on the narrow streets of the old fishing villages. Through the long years the fishhouses have faithfully served the men who battle the sea in quest of a living.

Waves

✿ ✿

THERE ARE POWER, majesty, and mystery in the waves that rhythmically break against the rocky headlands and the jutting granite arms or that slide slowly up the sandy beaches and dissolve in countless little bubbles and patterns of foamy lace. Down through the long ages of time, human beings have watched the waves of the ocean. In calm weather the gentle swells have a mesmerizing fascination. In a great storm one feels awesomeness and wonder as the surf crashes against the rocks and land and the angry waters hurl spume and spray high in the air.

Wind and water are perpetually at war with each other. The friction between them causes a series of risings and fallings on the ocean's surface. These are the swells that constantly play on the water, the movements that rock canoes and skiffs and dories. In average weather they come in a rhythmic series of alternate troughs and ridges, and one can adjust his body to them. When sharp winds blow up a squall, as it's usually called, the regularity is broken and, as a result, small boats are often overturned.

Fortunate it is for the coast line, for the harbors, and for the ships in the harbors that the great and violent waves of the open ocean lose much of their force before they attack. Great as the damage may be after lashing storms of the equinoctial period or after a screaming northeaster in winter, it would be infinitely greater were it not for the fact that the shelf that extends out into the ocean from land counteracts some of the power of the mountainous waves.

On a calm day the passing of a ship will cause undulations that extend for long distances. Oftentimes one sees rollers, though the water itself may be glassy in appearance and the sky clear.

This paradox is explained by the occurrence of a storm, sometimes a great distance away. Yet so mobile, so fluid is the water's surface, that these undulations may go on for mile after mile.

There's a fascination in waves. Both landlubbers and seafaring men can watch them hour after hour. On the quietest day there's some movement on the surface; in storms the ocean's might is fearsome to behold. Waves are an integral part of the appeal of the great waters for men and women who are drawn in spirit to the mystery of the sea.

American Eider Duck

❋ ❋

ALONG THE JAGGED COAST LINE of Maine can be seen the strikingly handsome American eider ducks. In small flocks they ride the swells near the shore; on calm, pleasant days they stand around on offshore rocks at low tide. The Latin name of this sea duck suggests a sizable, dignified bird, and *Somateria mollissima dresseri* lives up to his sonorous and impressive nomenclature. He is about 2 feet in length and has a wingspread of 3 feet or more. He is a bit heavy looking and somewhat cumbersome in flight, but his whole appearance is one of power and determination. As he flies, he has the unusual habit of holding his bill pointed slightly downward. Often small flocks fly in Indian file close to the water. They wind in and out along bays and inlets, rarely flying over land.

The male eider is a picture of sartorial contrast. He has a black underbody, black tail, and black crown, but his breast and back are snowy white. The lady is dressed in a demure outfit of brown and gray with flecks of black; in bright sunlight one can catch glints of cinnamon and buff. On rocky areas near the shore or on the islands close to the mainland, the female lays 8 or 10 delicately tinted, greenish-olive eggs. The nest is built of sea moss, grass, weeds, and occasionally a few small twigs. The lady lines the nest with down from her breast.

In the spring *Somateria* puts on an interesting display as he woos his ladylove. His notes are different from the ordinary quacks one expects from ducks. The tones seem to vary in key and volume, even as the human voice. As he tries to attract attention, he throws his head down; then he points his bill straight into the air and half rises from the water. Occasionally he flaps his powerful wings like a rooster.

The eiders are strictly sea birds. They do not care for salt marshes, drumlins, or the mainland above a narrow rim close to the ocean. As they dive for mussels, starfish, sea urchins, and periwinkles, they add their flavor to the life by the sea.

61

Gisela A. Ellis

Beach Grass

✿ ✿

BETWEEN OCEAN and mainland there is eternal battle. Every twenty-four hours the sea sends its charging waves of troops to assault earth and sand and rock. Every day it calls back the spent remnants of its force. Through the long years the warfare continues—never any armistice, never any quarter asked or given. Here and there along the coast line, between hard-packed beaches and the humus soil that nourishes tree growth, is that battleground of soft sand, the ever-changing dunes, where the beach grass makes its stand.

To anyone who is sensitive to Nature's complex and interrelated plan, there's something heartening about the sturdy clumps of growth. They are the doughty warriors who hold the battle-line ramparts. The wiry, tough stalks grow in bunches from the sand. Sometimes the clumps are in close formation; sometimes they are sparsely scattered over a wind-blown area. In the spring new shoots push up to the light from among the winter-bleached brown blades. Last year's slender, pointed blooms are still stiffly erect, spires that make a pattern against the sky line when one looks up to the dunes' crests.

Occasionally, when the lashing waves have thrown hammer blows at escarpments and have chiseled the sand away to horizontal, symmetrical ridges, the long, tenuous roots of the grass clumps above lie exposed to sun and air. Sometimes great storms hurl layers of additional sand over the dunes, half burying the grass. Now and then in winter, frost-crusts wrench the close-packed crowns asunder. The beach grass takes the weather as it comes, and when winter is past for another year or a storm has retreated for a time, it gathers its strength and sends more roots deep into the sand. It is a humble plant, standing faithful guard in the battleground between ocean and land.

Harbor Seals

THERE IS something grotesque yet peculiarly appealing about these "little old men of the sea." Their large, wide-spaced, innocent eyes have a poignant sadness, as if they were trying to figure out the tangled skeins of contemporary goings on. *Phoca vitulina*, however, is a philosopher of the first order. His attitude of resigned wonderment fits well with his calm, unhurried actions.

He is a member of the group of hair seals that are occasionally found as far south as New Jersey. Years ago a reef of rocks in New York harbor was called Robins' Reef because of the large herds of seals that gathered there. The word "robin," or robyn," is the Dutch name for seal, and the Amsterdamers logically labeled the seals' roost in their own language. The harbor seal definitely does not care for smooth beaches and sandy stretches. He likes to live near the coast where rocks and ledges abound.

His coat is nearly as variegated in color as Scotch plaid. When a group is lolling in the sunshine on rockweed-carpeted rocks, there is a beautiful symphony of blended colors. Some seals are almost white with shadings and markings of silver; others are a soft yellowish gray with dots and blotches of sooty black; still others have dark-gray backs and sides of orange hue. Occasionally there's one so spotted that his coat reminds one of a leopard. The five-toed flippers are strangely small for animals that weigh up to 200 pounds and may be 5 feet in length. Their short, stumpy, V-shaped tails make them look slightly ludicrous as they slither and wiggle from the rocks to the water.

One of the appealing sights along the northern rocky coast is a group of baby seals playing in the water at the edge of a sand bar. The little seals twist and turn and flip about like a litter of puppies, while the parents benignly watch or doze on the rocks above. There's an almost human quality about the seals, with their intelligent, questioning expressions. They are a distinctive part of the ocean's flavor to those who like to study the fauna along the coast.

Marsh Hawk

❋ ❋

SOON AFTER April's ruffled weather has been overcome by the loveliness of the fifth month, *Circus hudsonius* will be seen putting on an act that matches his scientific name. His hunting ground is the marsh and salt meadows, with an occasional foray over the dunes. He is a familiar friend to shoremen and seamen and is variously called marsh hawk, bog hawk, mousehawk, frog hawk, or snake hawk. He is a little larger than a crow. His coloring is the lightest of the hawks in the northeastern region— smoky gray on his back, almost white underneath, with dull black tips on his powerful flight feathers. His mate is a rich reddish brown on the upper body, a faded tannish brown beneath. They build their seasonal home in the higher reaches of the marshes, on the shrubby drumlins, or on high land above the edge of salt meadows. Here in May the lady lays five to eight plain grayish-white eggs.

Circus hudsonius is admittedly one of the smaller, plebeian members of the hawk clan, but there's something about the fellow that blends with the spirit of the marshes and the ocean's edge. Hour after hour, through sunny days and gray, he circles and twists over the level areas. Often he sails for a few moments, but more than half the time he flaps along in an unhurried but buoyant manner with powerful wings slanted at an upward angle from his shoulders. He may course back and forth over a small area for an hour, then suddenly head off along the shore line. Or on some hot July day he will begin spiraling upward, and hundreds of feet above earth he will float round and round in wide circles, riding the high air currents with almost motionless wings.

If one is fortunate, he may see the courtship flight in early spring after the birds have returned from their winter sojourn. A pair of marsh hawks flies close together to a great height. Then the male suddenly plunges downward, falling in a straight line for a few moments. In a trice the straight fall is broken, and he

65

puts on his aerial exhibition, turning a complete forward somersault. Occasionally he turns over and over a dozen times before he straightens out and bounces upward. On a warm, sunny day in May he may keep up this performance for hours.

Circus hudsonius is a conscientious head of his family. Except for a periodic trip of an hour or two along the coast to break the day's monotony, he is in faithful attendance. He helps build the nest; he takes a turn sitting on the eggs during the incubation period. After the young have hatched, he is a tireless hunter. As he comes to the nest with the prey in his claws, his shrill, piercing cry shatters the silence of a summer day. When he approaches, his mate leaves the nest and rises in the air. He releases the food; she catches it in her claws in mid-air and returns to the nest. He may circle a moment over his home and then dart off to resume his task. The passing of the food from mate to mate is one of the interesting sights of the bird world.

When September's first chills lay a warning hand on the land and water, the autumnal migrations begin. Groups of the hawks gather and take tentative wheeling flights over the browning grasses. In flocks of varying size they leave for the Southland at irregular intervals during September and October. Then on a day in November when one is standing on the marsh edge, he realizes the poignancy of the closing year. No longer are the graceful birds skimming over the grass tops or climbing into the sky. The last of the marsh hawks have left, and winter follows close behind.

Summer Ocean

✿ ✿

THIS IS the season of year when the ocean's belligerency is soothed for a brief interlude and a mood of quietness relaxes the tension that marks the battle between sea and land. It is now midway between the great tides that assault the earth at the full of the moon in spring and fall. Now the tides wax and wane in rhythmic flow, answering the mysterious call of Diana's power over the waters that cover the deep valleys between continents.

In the early morning gray-white clouds of fog hang over the harbors and coves, blotting out the rocky headlands, making beaches places of mystery, filling the hollows among the dunes, and spreading white blankets over the marshes. Moment by moment as the sun climbs above the quiet waters, the slanting rays pierce the banks of moisture and the spars of ships make soft etchings against the growing light. As the tides ebb and flow, the little froth-fringed waves break on the smooth beaches and form patterns of white bubbles on the wet sand. Where the rocks come down to meet the sea, the waves break gently and murmur constantly among themselves as they alternately advance and retreat.

The ships come and go on the gentle swells. Seiners and draggers put out their nets. Men in sharp-prowed dories and small powerboats haul their lobster pots. The herring gulls wheel and turn, glide and drift. They ride the air currents above the waves, drop to the surface like plummets when they see food, and argue in plaintive, halfhearted fashion among themselves.

When sunset time comes, long shadows creep out from the wharves, fishhouses, and masts of schooners. The voices of the gulls die away, and night's peace drops on the great waters. This is the summer ocean—calm and brooding—nurturing its strength for the coming battles when Summer's gentleness retreats before Autumn's untamed scouts.

H. Armstrong Roberts

July in the Dunes

✿ ✿

THE SAND DUNES are the ramparts that stand between the ever-attacking ocean and the ever-resisting land. Bulwarks against the high tides, the dunes constantly shift and change. The winds of the four seasons carry waves of sand hither and yon. In certain spots the sands make new dunes; in other places they are carried away, and one sees the stumps of long-buried trees or perhaps the stark, lonesome skeleton of a schooner cast ashore in a winter gale of long ago.

July is a good time to see the beauty of the dunes. At high twelve of the year Nature is usually beneficent in mood. The sea-rocket plants between the line of high tide and the foothills of the sandbanks drowse through the hot days and dewy nights. Their pearl-gray leaves make little islands of foliage in the sea of inorganic particles. On the sides of the dunes are the clumps of beach grass, their timothylike blooms reaching high into the air. Perchance in a secluded clump one may find the nest of the spotted sandpiper.

On the leeward side of the dunes are the stretches of poverty grass, dotting the sand with their yellow five-petaled blooms and wiry, heathery stems. Beyond the second line of the sand fortifications are the little pools of water where the marsh mallow lifts its fragile blossoms, swaying gently back and forth as the tail end of the ocean breeze dips down into the hollows. Around the pools are thick clumps of tangled bayberries and little forests of gray birches and red pine where the meadow hens build their casual, twiggy nests. It's quiet and peaceful. High twelve of the year is here, and the dunes reflect the spirit of the season.

Peep-los

✿ ✿

ALONG THE SANDY BEACHES from the Carolinas to the St. Lawrence the piping plovers make their homes. Their sad, gentle whistles remind one of the plaintive poignancy of the wood pewee's calls. *Charadrius meloda* is one of the well-loved and familiar members of the wildlife family by the ocean. His folklore names are butterbird, clambird, peep-lo, and tee-o. The latter two are descriptive of his sweetly mournful song.

Peep-lo is an extrovert by nature and prefers the open, expansive beaches with rolling dunes behind for a line of defense. He is handsomely and distinctively dressed. His stubby, black, slightly curved bill resembles the snout of a rhinoceros and fittingly complements his plump, chubby body. He wears a black band across his broad forehead and a broad black scarf around his neck. His back has the peculiar tannish-brown shade of dry sand. His waistcoat is grayish white and when he circles over the beach, he shows the pure white feathers of his wings.

The piping plovers build their nests in sand hollows. Often they use bright pebbles and bits of shells as decorations or identifying marks. The eggs are gray-buff dusted with spots of darkish brown. Sometimes when a person is standing on a wide beach and a peep-lo suddenly appears before him dragging his feathers and pretending to be in distress, it is because he is trying to lead the intruder away from his domicile.

The beaches would not be the same without these handsome little birds. Running gracefully and swiftly along the wet sands or wheeling in flight at low altitudes, their black-and-white beauty and their muted, melodious piping add interest to the shore line.

Summer Sunset

* *

Now THE GREAT RED BALL drops low above the hills. The ocean stretches peacefully to the line that divides the water and the sky. Quietness rests on sandy beaches, rolling dunes, and grassy marshes. In little fishing harbors dories ride gently at anchor. Gulls slowly beat homeward to nesting sites, still now that day is ending. Far across the waters a trail of pearl-gray smoke marks the path of a coastal ship. Quietness falls gently on both land and sea.

Minute by minute the sun closes the gap between earth and sky. Groups of people gather on granite headlands, plank piers, and jutting promontories to watch the day's requiem. Purple, orange, scarlet, and gold are the colors above the sinking sun. As it drops behind the hill, there is a brief period of breath-taking beauty. Broad splashes of bright colors are thrown into the sky, lighting the land beneath.

Then the brightness slowly fades, but for long minutes there is beauty in the sky—a softer blending of colors, more satisfying perhaps than the stark emphasis before. The light blues and yellows and shades of bronze paint a pastel picture. Across the steel-gray water is a shimmering path of color reflected from the spot where the sun has dropped from sight. Sometimes across a bay the path leads from land to land.

Moment by moment the color lessens. Dusk pushes the last of daylight over the horizon. Stars break through the curtain above. Far up the coast the first flash from the lighthouse tears a rip in the gathering blackness. A night heron calls from its perch on a trap-net buoy. A summer day is ended. The peace and quiet of a summer night rest on the ocean.

71

Burton Holmes: Ewing Galloway

Evergreens by the Sea

STRETCHING BACK from the shore line are the serried ranks of the evergreens. In some places the pastures and fields slope gradually to the sea; in other areas the line between ocean and mainland is craggy and steep, and granite cliffs take the pounding of the tides that twice a day make rhythmic assaults. But irrespective of the geologic formation, there's something about the ocean that calls to the cedars.

Sometimes the ranks are thick, and they stride in close formation toward the water; sometimes the evergreens are spaced far apart—advance scouts ahead of the main body, exploring the land. Many of the fields and pastures now studded with the slender, pointed shafts of green were once used by man. Pioneers claimed the land when a new nation was being hewed from a virgin wilderness. For generations it served man's purposes. Then the fertile, stone-free soil of the West called; mills were established on rivers; young people left the rocky farms. Little by little the fields were given back.

Nature always reclaims her own as soon as the pressure of man's hand is lifted from her breast. Seeds from the evergreens' cones float through the air ahead of the grove or woods. If one comes to rest on a pocket of soil and the conditions of light, moisture, and heat are favorable, new life begins. A tiny root goes downward; a slender pale-green spike lifts its head to the sun. Year by year the little trees push themselves upward. Succeeding decades see newly formed ranks established. And when time has passed on and decades have become history, the evergreens by the sea make a beautiful picture. Slowly and inexorably the once open spaces are dotted with the green columns.

When man looks down from upland roads and sees the cedars by the sea, he is looking at a complete cycle. Once man cleared the land for his purposes. Now Nature is filling the vacant spaces. The evergreens by the sea are a page of history in a nation's still unfolding drama.

Launching a Trawler

✿ ✿

THERE IS excitement in the air on the day of a launching. This is the climax of months of labor in a small shipyard at the edge of marsh, river, or sheltered cove. Perhaps the days of half a year have been checked from Time's calendar since the long, heavy keel was jockeyed into position and the curved ribs began to sprout from its sides. Week by week men who have been building ships for half a century and more have brought the trawler into being. Clear-grained white oak and patient craftsmanship have made another ship ready to go down to the sea. The last details have been finished. The carriage that will help hold the vessel upright as it is launched has been built. The ways are coated with a thick covering of yellow grease.

From near-by fishing villages and from farms in the surrounding countryside, men and women, boys and girls gather to watch the event. Minute by minute the tension mounts. Old-timers express opinions and reminisce of ships built long ago. The time of launching is carefully calculated to meet the height of the tide. Workmen go over every important point for a final checking. The laughter and talk diminish.

As the climactic moment draws near, silence spreads over the cluttered yard. There's a rich, pungent fragrance compounded of tar, rope, lumber, and salt air. Men with sledge hammers knock the blocks from beneath the body. Four men, two to each crosscut saw, start sawing through the two planks that hold the ship from the calling sea. The sharp teeth make monotonous murmurs as the two saws work into the wood. Suddenly there is a sharp, staccato crack. The boat starts downward to the ocean. The christening bottle is swung. Swiftly the trawler gathers speed and cuts a furrow into the water. A cheer goes up. Another vessel is dedicated to its work on the ocean.

Cranberry Bogs

ONE COMES UPON cranberry bogs in the depressions of the sand dunes. Here, in miniature valleys a few feet above the line of high tide, is the birthplace of many of them. Some of the established bogs that have known a half century of seasons near the ocean are only a few yards in diameter.

To watch and study the beginning of a new bog is to know something of the wonder of Nature's processes. In a small, mossy, moist spot among the dunes a bird drops a cranberry seed. All winter it rests beneath snow and ice. Only where the green covering of moss is found will the seeds germinate. If conditions of moisture and sun are right, the hard shell of the seed softens and the miracle of life occurs. Slender, hairlike roots go downward to find a foothold in Earth's breast; a stem of green goes upward to air and light. That is the first season's growth.

Then, in the next and succeeding years, long lines of single soldier-file leaves creep out over the green carpet. Along the gray-green tendrils at intervals of 3 or 4 inches are the uprights. On these branches, in due time, appear the blossoms and the red fruits. Eventually the long tendrils and sturdy uprights turn woody and wiry. But now, at the beginning, the stems and leaves are soft and colorful. At the ends of the tendrils the gray-green horizontal stems become a cranberry-red color with flecks and splotches of soft green. The tiny immature leaves are a deep reddish purple on top, a soft gray-brown underneath.

Just two or three lines of tendrils from one seed in a little depression among the dunes are the beginning. Red pines, gray birches, tangles of bayberry, fringes of marsh mallow, and dark purple blooms of blackjack grass encircle the spot. The newborn cranberry vines stretch their arms and take possession of a bit of the earth's surface.

Widow's Walks

✿ ✿

ALONG THE COAST LINE of the Northeast can be found the picturesque widow's walks—in villages of Cape Cod, on the salty island of Nantucket, by the granite-fringed coast of Maine, and on the hillsides of river towns that form a link between the mainland and the sea. Long years ago when great wooden cargo ships, sturdy whalers, and taut-lined clippers held spreading canvases to the winds and cut furrows in the waters of the oceans, the captains and owners used part of their trading profits to build square colonial homes. They were spacious and dignified houses, in keeping with the character of the men who sailed far and wide to the distant parts of the world. They were built by honest craftsmen. Most of the captains wanted their homes on a rise of land where, between trips, they could see the ocean from their windows. And on the spacious, gently sloping roofs they built platforms and surrounded them with railings and carved posts. Many a man climbed to his roof in those bygone days and held a glass to his eye, scanning the ocean that he had mastered, watching for the sail of a friend's ship coming back from the Orient, or watching a sail dip out of sight below the distant horizon.

No one knows when the term "widow's walk" was given to the roof-top lookout. There's heart-tugging poignancy in the words, for the ocean has taken great toll of the men and ships that have gone down to the sea. In generations past, fearful wives and mothers have spent long hours waiting and watching for overdue ships. Sometimes they never returned, and the lookouts became sanctuaries where broken hearts kept tryst with those who had gone. Memorials to the hopes and fears, joys and sorrows of yesteryear, the widow's walks are part of the flavor of the sea.

The Lobster

A LOBSTER is a strange creature. Among all the complicated forms of marine life there is none more interesting. With compound eyes on the ends of stalks, two slender orange-red antennae, four pairs of legs, a pair of huge pincers, a colorful body, and a beautiful fanlike tail, he looks like a miniature model of some grotesque and fantastic beast that roamed the shore line when the earth was young.

Homarus americanus is both carnivorous and vegetarian. In common with most forms of crustaceans and fish he is also a cannibal. His cosmopolitan appetite welcomes fish, eelgrass, shellfish, and the algae that cling around rocks. The big cruncher claw with rounded, white bony teeth holds the food; the tearer claw with its white-tipped, scarlet-red teeth rips the food into pieces for the forklike "fingers" to press into the mouth. The huge cruncher claw may be either on the right or on the left; hence the term left-handed lobster is correct although city folk think they are being jollied along when a leathery old lobsterman uses the expression.

The lobster's disposition is not the type that wins friends and influences people; but in spite of his touchy temper there's something appealingly individualistic about him. He can swim if necessary, even in reverse, but he prefers to crawl along the ocean shelf that slopes seaward from the land's edge.

There's a gorgeous symphony of rich colors in the armor of lobsters. Some are dark blue, black, green, or purple—and all shades in between. Others are fundamentally tan and brown and yellow with mottled darker blotches. There's a red horn with an ivory tip on the end of the nose, and similar-colored bony points are studded on the elbows and on the undersides of the claws.

Homarus americanus is different. That is part of his appeal. Those who are partial to lobster in all its varied forms say he is one of the best harvests the ocean yields to help feed mankind.

The Hermit Crab

✿ ✿

THE CRAB FAMILY has some distinctive traits. Its pugnaciousness and chip-on-the-shoulder attitude have brought it a degree of disrepute. But even if the term "crabby" is applied to certain members of *Homo sapiens,* it is a fact that the order Decapoda and suborder Brachyura have many interesting traits and quirks.

One of the individualistic members of the family is the hermit crab. He's a peculiarly long-sterned little fellow who gets his name because he takes the shell of a periwinkle or a snail for his home. He bears a slight resemblance to a miniature lobster with his large crusher claw and his smaller tearer claw, his two long antennae, and his curving tail. But the hermit has no armor to protect his soft-fleshed abdomen. Probably that is the reason why he makes his home in a shell. On the end of his tail are two hooks that give him firm anchorage. Anyone who tries to pull the little fellow from his home will discover the tenacity of his grip.

One of the interesting points about him is that the legs on one side are larger than those on the other. The spiral shells he preempts for homes are heavier on one side than on the other. Thus, as he has walked about through the aeons of time that crabs have inhabited the shore line, Nature has exerted her laws of adaptation and has developed the longer and stronger legs. Even his eyes are on stalks of uneven length so that as he waddles along one-sidedly both of them are on a level.

Hermits are common everywhere along the coast—on the beaches, along the marshes, under rocks and driftwood, in the tidal pools and dim apertures of the cliffs at the sea's edge. They are always in a hurry, trundling along with their portable homes. They molt frequently as they increase in size and hence must often find new shells. On a summer day, when one of them is in a rush to find a new home, he scurries around investigating one shell after another. It's only a temporary home he's seeking, but he's particular. He inspects many shells; he explores with

79

his long feelers; he seems to scrutinize them with his snappy eyes. When he does finally find the one that meets his requirements, he pops from the home on his back, wiggles quickly into the new domicile, and closes the opening with the larger claw. The hermit is a funny little fellow, always busy, pugnacious, and scrappy, but at least he never has a housing problem.

Beach Peas

✿ ✿

BETWEEN THE RESTLESS OCEAN and the soil that gives man his food are, in many places, the ever-changing dunes. Created by wind and water, they never know fixation, for the forces that brought them into being are constantly shifting the patterns. One wonders at the plants that find sustenance in the sands, at the beauty of the growing things that through the centuries have been subjected to such a harsh environment. Of them all, the fragile beach peas most nearly resemble garden plants.

The blossoms that open in early summer are blue-violet in color with traces of purple. The folded buds, set tightly against each other on the stem, open in regular procession. The succulent soft stem, green in shade, has beautiful streaks of reddish brown when it comes through the sand. There's a mottled effect among the streaks, like miniature dots, that reminds one of a rhubarb stalk. The leaf, shaped like the speckled alder, is a thing of beauty. Held against the light, it shows an irregular pattern of veins. The main vein may detour a bit to right or left from the base to the leaf's sharp-pointed tip. Around the outside edge there's a narrow vein of orange-pink tinge. The main vein with its side shoots resembles the vaselike American elm in winter without its foliage. The intricate pattern of the smallest veins reminds one of the links of finely wrought stainless-steel chains.

How does the beach pea survive the heat of summer in the sands? During hot days it holds its leaves upright, presents the edges to the sun, and thus holds down evaporation. But when the sun drops toward the horizon and coolness and moisture fill the air, the leaves relax toward the horizontal and absorb life-giving water. For a brief spell in early summer the beach peas are in bloom on the shifting sands. Their blue-purple blossoms and deep green foliage make a pattern of beauty for anyone who lets his eyes drop to the humble plants that live in the dunes.

Gisela A. Ellis

Trawling

❀ ❀

For COUNTLESS CENTURIES men have gone out to sea in ships to catch fish. For an unknown time before man began pushing a dugout along the ocean's edge, before he learned to use paddles and then sails of woven reeds and rushes to harness the wind, he built traps, or weirs, of stone and brush along the shore to reap a harvest from the sea.

Perhaps it was that quality called Yankee ingenuity that caused the early settlers to devise more efficient means by which to catch ground fish. Instead of fishing at the shore's edge with line or spear or depending on the schools of fish to swim into the weirs, they built boats and went out to sea in search of the places where fish gathered in great numbers.

That brought the heroic era of the schooners that fished the Grand Banks. They used trawls and hand lines set from dories. Time was when several hundred schooners operated from eastern ports. Today there are a baker's dozen or less. Eight or ten men on a trawler, or dragger as it's usually called, can catch many more fish in a shorter time by dragging a net along the bottom of the ocean. Furthermore, the eight or ten men share the profits that used to be divided among twenty or thirty.

When the captain has reached the spot he wants to fish, the net goes overboard. It looks very much like a kite. It is wide at the opening and narrows down toward the rear end. Floats suspend the upper edges; the bottom edge sinks. The rollers attached to the bottom edge bump along the rough, uneven floor of the ocean as the trawler moves slowly ahead at 4 or 5 miles an hour. Into the small, stockinglike end section go the fish—if luck is good. As the net fills with fish, the drag, or pull, on the ship gets heavier. The cables strain taut, the Diesel engine drones louder and louder. The propeller whips up a frantic splurging. The draggers usually work in the same direction as the tide because they can cover more ground. Also experience has shown that more fish are caught when dragging with the tide, because the fish are headed against it. Thus the fish go head on into the net instead of being scooped in tail first.

A common length of time for draggers to operate before hauling the net aboard is one hour. That means the net has scraped along 4 or 5 miles of bottom. Pulling the net in with the winch is a mechanical matter. When it is hauled aboard, the knot at the small end is untied and everything in the net is dumped on the deck. The net is thrown overboard immediately, the ship plods ahead, and all hands turn to sorting, dressing, and packing the fish into the holds, where they're kept on ice until the boat reaches market. Each variety of fish goes into a separate pen.

Fish is food. It is sold fresh, canned, frozen, salted, as fish cakes, and as canned chowder. It goes by truck and airplane to inland cities of the nation. There would not be the generous supply there is if seafaring men had not devised trawling to scoop in the ocean's waiting harvest.

High Tide in the Marshes

TWICE EACH DAY the pull of the sun and moon sends the waters of the sea against the land, and twice the ocean calls back into its depths the waves that it sent forth. When the sun and moon are in conjunction or opposition, as at new moon and full, the combined strength produces greater-than-usual tides.

The crest of water is most spectacular when a northeaster combines with high tide to hurl great waves at rocky shores or to throw the surging, froth-fingered windrows of water high on the sandy beaches. Then the sea demonstrates its awesome power, and never again in all eternity will that stretch of land or rock be just the same as it was before. But for anyone who loves Nature in quieter mood, there's beauty and a sense of fulfillment as August's quiet tides flow into the marshes.

Minute by minute the water creeps higher in the soft, muddy creeks that wind in and about the marsh areas. Soon the long waving ribbons of eelgrass are covered. Then the water reaches the level of the low-banked creeks and begins to spread out among the sturdy brown-sheathed canes of the thatch grass. There's no sense of urgency or display of power. Hot summer sun beats down on the quiet ocean; marsh hawks sail high on motionless wings, riding the slow currents of air. The climbing waters crawl higher minute by minute. So slowly do they rise that one hardly realizes when the moment of climax arrives. Then, suddenly, he senses the fullness of the marsh. Gray-green liquid has filled all the creeks and sloughs; it has spread over the lower areas and has almost reached the marshy meadows where only the great tides of spring and fall carry their water. In August the ocean is usually in benign mood. High tide in the marshes is a demonstration of the sea's power, but in the eighth month there is a brooding spirit of peace over the calm, grassy stretches that lie between land and ocean.

George French

Building Wooden Ships

✿ ✿

AT SCATTERED PLACES along the sea's edge the stark outlines of ribbed frameworks make patterned silhouettes against the sky, marsh, and water. Patient craftsmen still use adz, mallet, and saw to build wooden vessels in old shipyards of the Northeast just as they did long before the star of a new nation was born in the hearts of pioneering men and women.

The greater portion of the labor is done by hand. With cant hook and pole the long, heavy oak keel is edged into position on peeled rollers. Day by day the strong curved ribs grow along the keel. With razor-sharp, short-handled adzes men patiently hue the ribs to the correct curve, readying the framework for the oak planks. The end posts are fitted to the keel and made secure. When the solid planks are in place, holes are bored through them and deep into the ribs. Long wooden pegs are still used to hold the covering to the frames—as they were in days of long ago. With measured, rhythmic blows of chunky wooden mallets the pegs are driven home and then are sawed off flush with the planks. Cabins, bunks, and holds for storing the sea's yield are built into the ship. From a staging on either side men tamp long strands of tarred oakum into the cracks between the planks. Then the coating of paint is spread to protect the wood against the water that will be the ship's home.

The builders of wooden ships work carefully and unhurriedly. Human lives depend on their craftsmanship. Month follows month and gradually a ship comes into being and develops its own personality. No one knows when the first wooden ship was fashioned for man's use. A long, long time ago men learned to hew timbers and planking. A long, long time ago they hoisted sails to catch the power of the wind. Now the men who go out in trawlers use the power of engines, but the wooden ships still serve their needs.

M. P. Mims

Lobster Buoys

✿ ✿

SMALL, WEATHER-BEATEN SHANTIES nestle close to the rocky shore line of protected fishing coves along the coast. They crouch on gray, splintery piers where high tides sway the olive-green rockweed twice a day. On these humble little houses of the lobstermen the chances are good that colorful buoys are hung —over the doors and above the windows.

Each man has his own distinctive color pattern for his buoys. Some are solid colors—blues, reds, tans, and browns—but most are combinations of two or more colors. They are made in various shapes—rectangular, square, six-sided, and eight-sided—and are fashioned of red or white cedar, long-lasting wood to resist the salt water of the sea. Most of them have light-colored handles that stick above the water so the lobsterman can quickly spot the locations of his pots as he rows his steep-sided dory along.

The grizzled, sea-weathered men plan to keep a supply ahead, for ever and anon the ocean whips up its wrath and sends a northeaster to lash the land. Then many pots and buoys are destroyed. On stormy days of late fall and winter they sit around the little cast-iron stoves in their shanties, fashioning more buoys and painting them the colors that they have chosen. Summer folk come to the little fishing villages and exclaim over the quaintness and local color. They paint pictures and take photographs of the buoys on the shanties.

The lobster buoys are part of man's livelihood. They have played an important role in the drama of life along the coast. The colorful pieces of wood are the honorable vocational badges of men who go down to the sea to help get food for a nation.

Stake Driver

THE UPPER EDGE of the salt marshes—the belt of the blackgrass zone—is a favorite spot of the American bittern. This narrow strip, the last rampart between the ocean and the mainland, is reached by water only in spring and autumn when the great semiannual tides come with the full of the moon. Here the stake driver lays claim to a certain section. He and his mate build a rough nest of coarse reeds, a bulky affair that looks like a pile of brush. The female lays from three to six bluish-white eggs, and while she broods and later hunts for food, the stake driver acts as sentry.

Bitterns are notable for two reasons. When a man comes poking along through the heavy reeds of the 6-foot-high thatch grass, approaching from the ocean side, they "freeze" in position. One can almost step on them, so perfectly do they match the brownness of the protective environment. With long necks and bills pointed upward they stand for minutes without motion. When they finally move as one approaches very closely, they skulk off among the grasses, barely leaving a ripple in their wake.

But it's for the "stake driving" and "pumping" that they are most distinguished. There's no noise quite like it in Nature. The male bittern gulps air six to ten times with his head held high. Then he begins his song. As he makes the harsh noise, he moves his head from side to side and up and down. Some claim the hollow, raucous noise is similar to that made when a farmer drives a stake with a wooden mallet; others say it sounds like an old-fashioned wooden pump in operation. On a summer evening when the wide marshes are peaceful, the distinct, booming thump-thumps carry far on the moist air. *Botaurus lentiginosus* isn't handsome, but he adds life and interest to the marshes.

Sea Rocket

✿ ✿

STURDY AND TENACIOUS, these small green plants are the last outposts of land vegetation. There's an indefinable appeal about them as they keep their lonely vigil on the battle-scarred lines between the reach of high tide and the beginning of the sand dunes. When the great tides at full of moon in spring and fall send their frothing waves against the ramparts of the dunes, the sea rockets bow back and forth with the rushing waters; but unless a storm stirs the high tides to unusual bitterness, the little green plants hold their positions.

In many places along the coast there's a considerable stretch of sand between the line of high tide and the windrows that mark the beginning of the dunes. The sea rockets grow singly, in small clumps, or occasionally in closely packed sizable areas. There is beauty in the humble plants. The surface of the pinnate leaves is a frosty gray-green color; the backs are a soft pearl gray. When a wind whips in from the east or north, the constantly moving leaves remind one of waving human hands. The main stem, whitish gray on the outside and soft and velvety to the touch, is a beautiful shade of light green inside. It is succulent and filled with moisture, a life-giving reservoir if long weeks of heat and little rain come in the summer months.

In midsummer lilac-colored flowers appear. Their four petals are sometimes called "The Sign of the Cross," for the sea rockets are members of the family *Cruciferae*. When the hot sun beats down on them and the voice of the ocean is a monotonous murmuring, one doesn't appreciate the fact that here on the sands the thick, leathery-leaved plants are guardians of a battle line. In the mysterious workings of Nature the sea rocket was fashioned for a task. Over the years it stands faithfully at its sentry post.

George French

Net Mending

JUST AS FARMERS have their rainy-day jobs waiting for them in the comfortably cluttered, aromatic farm shops, so the men who go down to the sea have their work waiting when, for one reason or another, they are not out on the ocean. Sometimes it's more than spare-time work, for the men who tend trap nets along the shore, those who go seining for mackerel, and those who go trawling for ground fish along the rough floor of the ocean may meet with trouble. Then they are forced to take time out to mend nets.

Occasionally a trawler's net catches on rocks or on uncharted sunken ships; porgies get into the trap nets and slash the tar-coated twine; seines catch on obstructions, and frequently bigger fish than mackerel get into them and rip and tear the strands. A shark or swordfish can cause many hours of work.

All along the shore line from early spring until late fall, on the old granite piers and wooden wharves, on the steps in front of old fishhouses, and on the headlands that jut out into the water, one can see the net menders at work. The artists who flock to the fishing villages in summer exclaim at their quaintness and proceed to set up easels and to paint them.

But there is nothing quaint about net mending to the men who depend for their living on trapping or catching fish in the sea. True, it is a job that an elderly, horny-handed fisherman can do when his days of active fishing are over, and that is the reason why so many men of threescore years and more can be seen sitting in the sun and skillfully tossing the wing-tailed shuttle back and forth as they knit new sections into the seines, gill nets, and trap nets.

It looks easy, but it's as deceptive as some of the knitting Grandmother used to do on thumbs and heels. In mending a tear, the unnecessary tag ends are cut off, then enough additional strands are deliberately cut to fulfill requirements. The end of the new twine must start at a knot joining three strands

93

or from a tag end leading from such a knot. The weaving, or mending, must end at a similar point.

If a net has a large hole in it, then the common practice is to patch it with a section from a discarded net. That is the reason why one sees old nets piled up in the weather-beaten fishhouses along the coast. A fisherman needs his "attic" just the same as a farmer needs a scaffold where odds and ends of materials can be kept for making repairs.

On sunny days the net menders work outdoors. In stormy weather they sit in the gray-shingled fishhouses. In winter the old rusty stoves make the shacks cozy. Mending nets is part of the fishing business. As a man watches the calloused fingers of a grizzled old-timer at his task, he senses that this is the way fishermen through the long ages have prepared their equipment to go down to the sea for a part of man's food.

Nighthawks above the Marshes

✿ ✿

ON THE EDGE of a marsh meadow on a calm moonlit evening in July one can hear the nighthawks playing their bass horns. They are not classified with the birds that haunt the edge of the sea, yet they are common in the fields and upland stretches above the ocean.

Chordeiles virginianus and his mate are the most casual house-keepers. The lady often lays her two gray-and-white mottled eggs on rocks, ledges, or·bare ground. After the eggs hatch, however, both parents are conscientious providers. It is an amusing and interesting spectacle in the early evening to see one of the parents light near the drab-colored youngsters, walk awkwardly to one, and push his offering of food into the baby's mouth. The nighthawk is far from handsome, but his conservative cloak, white throat muffler, white bars on his tail, and white patches on his long slim wings give him a certain air of distinction. He always perches lengthwise on a limb, a rail, or even a telephone wire.

It is a unique experience on a summer night to listen to the nighthawks' booms. They sound with startling clearness in the semidarkness as the birds drop vertically—and recover. The eerie bass note, which is caused by air rushing through the wings' primary feathers, blends with the spirit of the lonesome marshes.

Evening is the time when the nighthawks wheel and circle, climb and dive. Perhaps a distant lighthouse ticks off its periodic dashes, buoys lift warning gleams in harbor channels, and occasionally a night heron's reverberating booms punctuate the silence that rests over the spreading expanse. Nighthawks above salt marshes in summer darkness are part of the flavor of the strip between ocean and land.

August Sea

THE EIGHTH MONTH brings with it low twelve of the ocean's annual cycle. The calm, sultry stickiness of dog days rests over the land and broods over the quiet sea. It's the time of lowest tides, and the gray-green-blue water stretches almost motionless to the hazy and blurred horizon's rim. Twice in each day the waters rise and halfheartedly slither up the fine-sand beaches or break lackadaisically against granite headlands. The water pushes up the creeks that wind through the marshes. The eelgrass at low-tide mark waves languidly back and forth. Twice in each twenty-four hours the sea calls its sluggish legions back into camp.

Along the shore men go out at dawn to pull their lobster pots and lift the trap nets to see what harvest they have reaped. The heavy white fogs reluctantly loose their holds on coves and bays, inlets and beaches, and finger rays of sunlight strike reflections on the steel-gray water. Herring gulls begin their daily search, complaining peevishly of scant pickings. A few night herons quawk intermittently as they wing their way heavily to the red pine groves in the lee of the dunes.

Through long sunny hours the glassy sea ripples listlessly, for never is the ocean quiet. On the calmest days there's always an eternal restlessness—a warning of its power. At day's end the sun lays a golden carpet on the glinting surface, and spectacular colors light up the clouds above the point where the red ball drops from sight. Dusk lingers for an interlude, fading into darkness as the day's curtains are drawn. Lights flash from the headlands to guide sea travelers on their way. August's night calm settles on the wide waters.

Starfish

✿ ✿

MANY DEFINITIONS in the book of words would make more illuminating reading. That of the starfish, or *Asterias vulgaris*, is tersely scientific: "Any of numerous echinoderms having a body of radially disposed arms (usually five)." To understand *Asterias* one must know that an echinoderm is an animal, not a fish. The Greeks have the name for it: "echinos" means urchin, and the suffix "derm" signifies skin.

The starfish dwell along the ocean's edge in the area below the line of low tide. They are colorful animals of green, blue, orange, yellow-tan, and purplish red. The upper sides of their arms and the backs of their bodies are covered with whitish dots. They remind one of Grandmother's sugar cookies dotted with caraway seeds.

The underside, or stomach, of the *Asterias* is an interesting arrangement. Under the microscope one can see the hundreds of suckers, or feelers, open-ended appendages that pull him in the direction he wishes to go. When he's hungry, he humps himself over a mussel and forces open the shell. His legs pull from their sockets very easily, but like the lobster, he can grow others within a year.

He's not high in society, just one of the plebeians of marine life that can only distinguish darkness from light through sensitive spots that serve as eyes at the end of each arm. He moves about at high tide, eating old and dead sea animals, and pays his way by helping to keep the ocean clean. At low tide he hides in the ledges and holes along the shore. The colorful star-shaped little fellows add interest to any study of Nature's myriad forms of life along the water's edge.

Beacons of Faith

✧ ✧

ON LONELY ISLANDS along the coast, on craggy headlands that jut into the ocean, and above sand bars that twist through shallow waters stand tall towers that fling their beacons into the darkness, reminders that the sea still takes its toll. At irregular intervals it gathers its awful strength; wind and water combine in fury and lash its surface without mercy. Perhaps a vessel is driven onto the sands or against jagged cliffs; here and there one sees them—gaunt, weather-silvered frames silhouetted against the dunes or smaller, moss-covered sections wedged tightly into tide-washed crevices.

To men on ships at sea lighthouses are more than indications of location. Primarily, it is true, they serve a utilitarian need. They point the course for coastwise vessels; to travelers returning across the ocean they are often the first sign of homeland. But to a man on a ship there is more to a lighthouse than just the gold-red dots and dashes that intermittently slice the dark page of night.

A lighthouse is a man-built structure of rock and cement. In material terms one can explain the functioning of the gleams to which seafaring men have turned their eyes in calm weather and in gales. Standing on the shore or on the crest of a high dune on a soft summer night and watching the steady writing in the darkness, one can sense a little of what it means to sailors to see the messages pulsing rhythmically against the black curtain. The never-failing flashing codes are a symbol of a man's fidelity to the trust invested in him. To men on ships they are a lift and a reassurance in the glow in the darkness. Lighthouses along the coast are beacons of faith.

Common Terns

✾ ✾

LIFE ALONG the sea's edge would lose some of its summer savor without the terns. Common tern is his everyday name, but it fails by far to do him justice. Much more fitting are his three nicknames—mackerel gull, summer gull, and sea swallow. The latter is especially appropriate. The common terns circle and glide, climb and dip above the waters offshore, as do the barn swallows over daisy-dotted meadows and sidehill mowings of June grass.

The terns are handsome fellows with their black caps, gray mantles, reddish-yellow beaks with darkened tips, and orange-yellow legs. Many who watch a flock of them think they are small gulls. Each has two pointed black-edged feathers that form a V rudder similar to that of the swallow. When he is standing on the beach or mud flats, the folded wings extend beyond the tail's tip.

At intermittent intervals from May to October they play roles in an exciting drama. When schools of bluefish or mackerel come coursing along, they drive hordes of small fishes—"bait," as the fishermen call them—ahead. The small 6-inch and 7-inch fish are frantically trying to escape the larger ones. The little fish, by the tens of thousands sometimes, break water and seem almost to skip over the waves. Often the surface of the water is a churning dark gray mass. Circling terns see the small fish. Screams suddenly rend a summer afternoon's quietness. In a few moments the alarm has gone out and hundreds of the black-headed gulls are flying over the bait. It is an aerial circus for a time. The terns' raucous screams fill the air. They whirl and bank and climb. They plunge like arrows straight down into the water, closing their wings tightly about their bodies just as they enter. They rise quickly, usually with fish. It is a memorable sight to see several scores of them climbing, poising a brief moment, and then plunging downward again. As they come from the water, they shake their feathers and all the time their wild, strident hunting cries make a bedlam. Then if, by chance, fisher-men see the spectacle, they quickly start their seining boats and head out to circle the mackerel or bluefish. The terns get their small prey, and if the god of luck is smiling, the fishermen get the larger fish.

If one has a chance to visit an island or a spot on the main-land where the *Sterna hirundo hirundo* nests, it is an experience never to be forgotten. He prefers open sands or rocky spaces to areas of vegetation. When Mrs. Tern decides the time has come to build her nest, it is but a moment's work. She settles on a sandy spot and scratches the dirt aside, much as a busy hen in a barnyard digs for worms. The tern faces in several directions as she scratches, and the sand flies from beneath her feathers. Sometimes the nest is a bare hollow in the sand. Occasionally it is a fairly sizable nest of grass and dried seaweed. Once in a while it looks as if it were a deliberate bit of camouflage under a clump of beach grass or at the edge of a thicket of reeds. The majority of the nests have three or four eggs but a considerable number have five or six.

The head of the family does most of the fishing for his mate and offspring. While the lady sits on the eggs, he keeps bring-ing her small fish. When one is watching a nesting area, it is easy to recognize her food call. It could not be considered mu-sical, but her plaintive, hoarse cry of hunger is much different from her rough, fighting screams when she is attacking a school of fish. As the mate approaches with a fish dangling from its beak, she lifts her head and opens wide her mouth. Often, how-ever, another male will snatch the other end of the fish. Then, like two cock robins on a lawn at opposite ends of an earth-worm, the two terns stage a tug of war, pulling and yanking.

When the half-grown, ungainly youngsters are sprawling and lolling over the nest's sides, it's good for a chuckle to watch the feeding. The parent comes gliding in, and the fish in his mouth is no deterrent to his peculiar high-pitched but soft-sounding cry. The young birds go berserk with hungry anticipa-tion. They flip-flop about, fall, get up, flutter their wings, and hold their mouths wide open. The parent never seems to hesi-

101

tate. He selects one of his offspring, walks to it, and in a brusque, determined manner shoves the fish into the waiting cavity. After the young are able to fly, the parents apparently feed them for a few days on the wing until they learn to hunt for themselves.

The common terns are common birds in numbers. But from spring to fall their flashing white bodies and glistening black heads make striking pictures above the blue-green waters.

Deer in the Dunes

FROM THE FAR SOUTH to the extreme North, along the edge of the ocean named for the Greek god who upholds the heavens, there are areas of sand dunes fingering the coast. Sometimes these waves of wind-driven sand come close to the ocean and the high tides of the new and full moon sculpture strange patterns in the escarpments. Occasionally, due to freakish actions of the winds, extensive areas of dunes lie behind wide-spreading salt marshes where thatch grass waves gently to and fro.

In the dunes where islands of red pine, gray birches, and poplars provide hiding, the white-tailed deer make their homes. Sometimes these forested spots in the valley are almost as thick as jungle growth. Not only do the trees grow in close array, but the bayberry bushes make almost impenetrable thickets around them. A small, dense grove in the midst of bayberry ramparts may be the home of several deer. A few nature lovers, who have made the study of the dunes their hobby, know the deer paths that curve in and out among the sands. The deer have certain favorite places where they feed on the fox grass and spike grass near the upper edge of the marshes. They know the location of all the fresh-water pools in the vicinity.

Anyone who seeks the quiet beauty and loveliness of the dunes at dawn and sunset is often rewarded by glimpses of the white-tails as they wind slowly along to and from the feeding spots. Often there's a family party—buck, doe, and a fawn or two. In the dawn's growing light or as dusk is gathering its shadows, they present a picture of beauty. In the heart of day men and women, boys and girls may shout and play on the sides of the dunes, little realizing that a few yards distant, in the tangled thickets and close-growing trees, the deer are resting comfortably and safely. In the midst of man's activities the wild creatures have learned how to find a peaceful sanctuary.

103

Trap-netting

❖ ❖

SINCE BIBLICAL TIMES, and probably long before, we know that men have been getting a part of their food from the fish harvest of the sea. No man knows when it was discovered that fish were good food. Perhaps it was much longer ago than is commonly supposed. It may be that very early in man's history, when he was emerging as a distinct species, some brave individual reasoned that since the flesh of animals was improved by cooking over a bed of coals, then a fish from a near-by pond or stream might also be improved by similar treatment.

Neither does history record when the first man conceived the idea of a net for capturing fish. But this we do know: trap nets or floating nets have been used for hundreds of years. All around the world today in the latitudes suitable for fishing, men set their trap nets and make the daily or every-other-day trip in small boats to bring in whatever the harvest may be.

A trap net is a simple and efficient affair. A leader line runs from a spot near the shore to the mouth of the net. This leader line is an upright net from the surface of the water to the bottom. It is held vertical by a row of cork buoys at the top and by lead weights spaced every few feet along the bottom. Many schools of fish regularly follow along the shore line, and when they strike this obstruction, they swim along beside it, searching for the way around. Instead, it guides them to the conical opening of the trap net itself. At the rear end of this rectangular shape, held on the surface by wooden buoys and anchored at the corners with weights attached to kegs that float, is the "pocket." The pocket is the small area into which the fish are crowded before they are dipped into the boat.

Pulling the net is an interesting process. At early dawn three men go out to take the harvest. They have a small powerboat. A 16-foot dory is towed behind. At the trap the powerboat is fastened lengthwise beside the pocket. Then the men climb into the dory and start pulling the net at the other end. There's a man at the bow, another at the stern of the dory, and a man in the middle. As the men pull up the net, the fish are forced toward the pocket. The net that's pulled slides back under the dory into its former position. Minute by minute the fish are crowded closer to the powerboat—and then finally the mackerel, the squid, the pollack, and anything else are worked into the pocket.

Two of the men climb aboard the powerboat. The third stays in the dory, holding a section of the net above the water so the fish cannot escape from the pocket. On the powerboat one man takes a large net with a sturdy handle and dips it into the seething mass of fish. A strong rope runs around the bottom of the net and up to the top rim. Hauling and pulling on this rope, the men lift the fish on deck. This is repeated until all the catch is gathered from the pocket.

That's the harvesting end of trap-netting. It's what thousands of summer visitors see when they come to the old New England fishing villages. What the casual visitor doesn't realize is the other work connected with this method of fishing. Every two weeks the nets have to be lifted from the water and spread out to dry; otherwise the thread would rot away. Sometimes big fish get into the nets and rip and tear them; then they have to be mended. While some nets are drying or being mended, there must be others in the water.

Many, many dawns when the men go out the harvest is small. All men who take a living from Nature—fishermen, hunters, and trappers—know that the catch is unpredictable. But trap-netters still set their nets at the ocean's edge and hope for a bountiful harvest.

Marsh Mallow

✿ ✿

BEHIND THE FIRST few irregular lines of dunes, in the sheltered hollows where little pools are the center of life through the heat of summer, the lovely marsh mallow lifts its large-petaled blossoms above the quiet waters. The dune hollows are miniature worlds. Around them may be complete circles of barren sand, a part of the dune formation. But in the hollows, where humus soil has accumulated through the centuries, jack pines, gray birches, and bayberry bushes make a sanctuary for wildlife.

Tangled thickets of bayberries circle the little pools. Between the low-growing, almost impenetrable hedge and the water is a beautiful necklace of pink, rose, and soft reds during the heart of summer. On sturdy stalks from 2 to 4 feet high the hollyhocklike five-petaled flowers hold their beauty to the summer sun. The blooms are borne in clusters at stem terminals or from the leaf angles. The leaves are an unusual shade of light green—a coloring that has a tinge of violet and purple in the shadows of sunset.

Althaea officinalis is the largest of all wild flowers. The thick, bulgy root is used both by confectioners and by apothecaries. *Althaea* serves man's material needs, but to him who knows the interest and appeal of the small fresh-water pools among the dunes the areas are wild gardens of loveliness. Protected from the hot, dry winds, with moisture available for their roots, the masses of pink and rose petals are colorful spots among the tans and browns of the surrounding sands.

Stone Walls to the Ocean

✿ ✿

ANYONE WHO RIDES along the broken shore line of the Northeast will see an endless procession of stone walls. They are a part of New England, running along winding country roads, circling meadows and fields, climbing steep hillsides, and making lanes from barns to pastures. Over them lean alders, gray birches, and sumacs; beneath them woodchucks and chipmunks tunnel their burrows; on them partridges stand in spring and send whirring drum calls reverberating across the fields.

There's something poignantly appealing about the walls that stretch down to the sea. They make a cross-stitch pattern on the sloping countryside. The granite rocks are thick with green-gray lichens. In many places the old walls are heaved and tumbled by the frosts of long-ago winters. Occasionally they stretch down across the fields beyond the line of high tide.

Generations ago men came to this broken shore line where the sea and land meet so intimately. As soon as cabins and barns were built, they cleared the virgin soil for their corn and other crops. With stoneboats, oxen, and stout ash poles for levers, they worked at making land. The best of the soil went into fields for grain; the poorest went into pastures. But whether for pasture or for cropland, the fences were necessary. It was logical to make them of the stones and rocks left there some 25,000 years ago when the last glacier grudgingly withdrew toward the North.

Now the stone walls remain—memorials to those pioneers who began building a new nation because they had visions in their hearts of the integrity of man's spirit. Patiently they wait through the generations of time for the country, of whose history they are a part, to fulfill the dreams of men of long ago.

Black Skimmer

❋ ❋

THERE WAS A TIME when the black skimmers were common along the northern coast, but now they add interest to the coast line from New Jersey southward. When Champlain explored Cape Cod in 1605, he wrote, "We saw also a bird with a black beak, the upper part slightly aquiline, four inches long and in the form of a lancet; namely, the lower part representing the handle and the upper part the blade, which is thin, sharp on both sides, and shorter by a third than the other, which circumstance is a matter of astonishment to many persons, who cannot comprehend how it is possible for the bird to eat with such a beak. It is of the size of a pigeon, the wings being very long in proportion to the body, the tail short, as also the legs which are red; the feet being small and flat. The plumage on the upper part is gray-brown, and on the underparts pure white. They go always in flocks along the seashore, like the pigeons with us."

No question but *Rynchops nigra nigra* is a peculiar fellow. His folklore names—cutwater, scissorbill, and shearwater—give clues to the way he captures his food. With his powerful wings spread to 4-foot width, his forked tail serving as a rudder, he skims along close above the water. When he sees food, he keeps flying but lowers his bill into the water. Occasionally in the shallows he miscalculates the depth, and his red, black-tipped mandible snags on the bottom and flip-flops him into a grotesque tumbling act.

Rynchops and his mate are very casual in their homemaking. The eggs are deposited in the open sands. He's an interesting fellow to watch on a summer day, and his peculiarly nasal barking adds an off-tune medley to the music of breaking rollers.

Gisela A. Ellis

Tracks in the Sands

✿ ✿

MANY NATURE LOVERS have experienced the pleasure of reading stories in the snow—stories printed by animals and birds as they have gone about their business after a fresh fall of white has left a blank page. Fewer are they who know the joys of reading tracks along the beaches and in the dunes. Of course, if the sands are dry and the winds are blowing with any force, the spoor is quickly erased. But there are many days of the year when early morning hours offer good reading to anyone who likes to wander by the ocean. The oblique sunlight slanting across the sands deepens the shadows of the imprints and brings out fine details.

Very rarely will one see an animal; but if he takes a particular area of beach and dune for his regular beat, he will soon come to recognize certain tracks. Common ones are those of the Virginia, or white-tailed, deer. They live in the islands of red pines, gray birches, and bayberry bushes in the low spots among the dunes. Here they have shelter and water. Before dawn they go to feed on patches of grass, and often their sharp-edged footprints can be found in the wet sand of the shore. Occasionally the tracks show that a doe and her fawn came to the ocean's edge, stood quietly for a time, and then returned unhurriedly to the feeding spots in the dune hollows. Once in a while there's another story. The deer tracks are a tangled conglomeration of prints over half an acre in area. There are big, broad tracks that look as though a buck or two were in the herd; then there are the smaller tracks of the does and the tiny ones of the few-months-old fawns. Here the deer leaped and jumped and played. Some apparently sprang straight ahead as evidenced by angular cuts to the rear of the prints; others jumped sideways, and the slanting cut of their hoofprints to right or left confirms it.

Kooza, the red fox, inhabits the thickets of the dunes. Along the coast line in many areas he is the great enemy of rabbits and mice. One can tell Kooza's prints in the sand, as in the snow,

111

because of the two claws and toes that are in front. Foxes more commonly take their appointed rounds among the dunes and on the beach in the darkness of night, but upon occasion, if one is watching from the crest of a high dune, he will see Kooza trotting along in the hollows in full daylight, his big tail held aloft like a banner or straight behind like a rudder.

Muskrats sometimes travel over the dunes from one swampy place to another. If there has been a recent rain and the sand is moist, one can see the impression of their webbed hind feet. Swinging back and forth between the prints are the grooves made by their tails. In some places the grooves are deep; in others they are shallow. One can almost visualize one of the ungainly fellows plodding phlegmatically forward, his tail bouncing up and down behind him.

Mephitis, the striped skunk, is partial to the beach. He likes to wander down to the high-tide line and below to see what the waves have left. He's a beachcomber of the first degree. *Mephitis* probably doesn't object to clams and mussels, but according to the story his tracks tell, he is chiefly concerned with digging for grubs and worms. In soft, moist sand his spoor is easily read. Each toe and claw shows distinctly. *Mephitis* doesn't worry about enemies; he puts his feet down deliberately and forcefully.

One of the loveliest tracks in the dunes, especially beneath the beach grasses and on the sandy sides of hillocks above the bayberry thickets, is that of the white-footed mouse. Whitefoot is one of the most appealing of all small animals. In his soft gray coat, with beady black eyes and inquisitive, twitching nose, he always has an air of gentle bewilderment. Whitefoot lives in old rotting limbs of trees, in decaying stumps, and beneath piles of debris. The dense islands of red pines and gray birches in the dune hollows harbor many of his family. But out on the clean sands one can study his dainty tracks, which resemble miniature etchings. Occasionally Whitefoot is in a hurry to cross a patch of sand and he gallops along leaving his prints in groups of fours, very much like those of a rabbit.

There are other stories to be read in the tracks of pheasants, crows, sandpipers, gulls, rabbits, grasshoppers, and occasionally snakes. The unthinking man who comes to the dunes or stands on a lonely, uninhabited beach may believe the area is devoid of life. It looks bleak and barren. The gray-green sea stirs restlessly in its uneasy bed; the beach grass bends and writes hieroglyphics in the sands; and the gray birches and the red pines twist in the swampy hollows. Yet near at hand are many forms of animal and bird life. Each day, unless a storm is raging, they come out and leave their footprints on the sands, and anyone who wishes may read their spoor and learn much about their activities.

The Great Black-backed Gulls

✿ ✿

A GENERATION AGO the great black-backed gulls were rare along the northeastern coast. Now they are staging a comeback, and the big handsome fellows are often seen in company with the herring gulls. Oftentimes the latter are confused with *Larus marinus*. The herring gulls, *Larus argentatus smithsonianus,* have the more impressive name, but the blackbacks have the more impressive appearance. The big birds are called various names by the fishermen—minister gull, turkey gull, coffin bearer, and saddleback.

The blackbacks are, on an average, about a fourth larger in size than their cousins. The adults are about 2½ feet in length and have wingspreads of 5 feet or more. Their sooty-black backs make striking contrasts with their white heads, breasts, and tails. The large, hooked, deep yellow beaks are powerful tools.

Larus marinus has never studied books on etiquette. It tears and rips at its food. Of uneven disposition, it often turns robber and chases other birds until they drop their food. It destroys and eats small birds, ducklings, mice, and rats. It seems to take a diabolical delight in waiting until a group of herring gulls are having a feed on the rocks, and then it descends in wrath and drives the others away.

The great black-backed gull is not an appealing bird. It has not the airy grace of the herring gulls in flight. But the big birds are here again along the coast. They are part of Nature's plan to maintain the delicate balance among the species of life.

White Spruces by the Ocean

* *

ONE OF THE most beautiful trees of the northeastern coastal plain is the white spruce. Above rocky shores where fields and pastures slope down to the ocean, white spruces of all sizes stand like dark green inverted exclamation points. Where Nature is reclaiming the land once wrested from her by pioneers, they remind one of a marching evergreen army with small scouts advancing ahead of the main body. Here and there in pastures and fields are individual trees that tower 100 feet and more in the air.

Anyone who has been in the white spruce forests along the northern coast has a memory of beauty. In these groves the trees reach a height of 150 feet; the trunks may be 4 to 5 feet in diameter. The spaced trees, the murmuring canopy overhead, the dim light, and soft needle-carpeted aisles that stretch away make one think of the quiet dimness of a cathedral. *Picea canadensis* is a tree of both majesty and friendliness.

The leaves of this spruce have stripes of whitish dots on each of the four sides of the short needles. The small cones with their imbricated scales are borne on the tips of small twigs. *Picea* is peculiar in that it has no regular season for unlocking its cones and permitting the seeds to fly away on the wind. In January or in June one can usually find freshly opened cones on the ground beneath the tree. White spruces grow over a vast region of North America, but they have especial appeal where the northern land meets the ocean.

H. Armstrong Roberts

Spirit of the Marshes

THERE IS SOMETHING poignantly lonesome yet peculiarly appealing about the salt marshes. There are broad expanses that reach inland from the sea to the fields from which man gets his food; there are small marsh meadows that end abruptly against stony hillsides and cliff-seamed escarpments.

Some of the salt marshes along the Atlantic seacoast cover thousands of acres; others are small and intimate—grass-covered nooks and coves. Marsh creeks with soft, gray-black mud bottoms wind in and out. Their banks are often bare and eroded with small cuts and fissures where the power of the tide has eaten into them. Twice each day the ocean throws its waves far inland through the marshes. The sea's power both builds and destroys as the salt water follows the curving creeks back to the line of high tide.

Here and there on many of the larger marshes are the drumlins, low-lying glacial hills and hummocks left by the ice barriers. Some of them are small, a few rods long and wide; others are of considerable size. From a distance they remind one of massive prehistoric animals resting in the marshy terrain.

There are four definite levels to a salt marsh and each has its distinctive vegetation. There are only a few plants to learn because the blighting power of the salt water limits the extent of plant life.

Starting at sea level, there is the zone of the eelgrass. It is neither grass nor seaweed but a lowly member of the group of flowering plants. The blossoms are tiny, hidden at the base of the leaves. Eelgrass gets its name logically, for it waves like the bodies of eels. It grows in matted streamers at the sea-level mouths of the mud creeks. The long, ¼-inch-wide strips wave back and forth in the water, and in the sheltering dimness of the thick growth are countless crabs and eels, snails and sea worms.

Dead eelgrass is pulled to sea with the outgoing tides and is then brought back and cast on the beaches. Sometimes when a northeaster comes, it throws the windrows of dead grass high on the beach above the normal high-tide line, and in the shelter of the tangled dried grass the savanna sparrows build their nests. In the late fall farmers and fishermen gather the wiry material and pack it around their homes, just as inland countrymen pack their homes with sawdust, to foil the probing fingers of winter storms.

Above the eelgrass zone is the area claimed by the thatch grass. Its zone is from within 3 or 4 feet of low-tide level to ordinary high-tide level, and if, by chance, the ocean throws up silt and builds a section so high that average tides do not wash over it, then the thatch grass ceases to grow.

Thatch is an interesting grass. Often it grows to 6 feet or more in height, its jaunty plumes of tan-colored flowers and seeds waving in the breeze. It's a strong grass and helps build up the soil level of the marshes, for its tenacious roots and sturdy stalks catch and hold the soil particles washed in by the tides.

Since the days when the pioneers made their first homes along the seacoast, thatch grass has served man's needs. Farmers cut it at low tide to use as mulch for their plants and young trees; they stack it behind the barns as bedding for their cows and horses. Gardeners are still partial to it because it is free from weed seeds. Each spring the thatch-grass zone starts anew, for during the late autumn and in winter and early spring, the sheets of jagged ice flatten every spear of it.

Above the thatch-grass area is the zone of the marsh hay, or more properly, the salt grass. This section is called the meadow marsh by farmers who live close to the ocean. Only occasionally, perhaps once a month, do the tides flood this expanse. The surface of the meadow marshes is fairly firm. One can wander over the hummocky land and not be in immediate danger of sinking to his hips in mud, as he is in the thatch-grass zone. There are, to be sure, lower spots in the marsh-hay reaches—spots the farmers call sloughs. Each of the previous two zones has but one simple form of vegetation. Here, on the third level,

118

one can find three grasses—fox grass, spear grass, and spike grass. They grow from 10 to 15 inches high.

At the turn of the century, cutting marsh hay was a regular part of the summer's work with many farmers. It was usually done in August when the tides run lowest. The horses were equipped with flat, broad wooden shoes to help hold them on the surface. Mowing machines cut the swaths on the dried sections; groups of men with scythes mowed the wet places.

In olden days some of the marsh-hay areas were surrounded by wide tidal creeks, and the men floated horses and equipment across on homemade barges. Then the hay was piled on the boats and brought to the stacking places nearer the mainland. The hay was usually stacked on staddles, ends of oaken posts that were driven into the soil and extended a foot or so above the surface. There are still places up and down the coast where farmers harvest the marsh hay, and one can see the stacks, like pointed tents, dotting the wind-swept areas. In winter when the land is hard with frost, farmers go out with sledges and haul the hay to the barns. Many own their patches of salt marsh, though the home farm may be several miles distant. In the old deeds of their farms is written a right of way to get to the marsh. A large percentage of the marsh hay is suitable only for bedding, especially if it is out late; but if the season is favorable and the countryman can get onto his meadow marsh early in August, the fodder is good for dry cows and neat stock.

This third zone has a few lovely flowers that lift their blossoms in season to the hot summer sun. The glasswort, inconspicuous among the grasses in summer, puts on a cloak of flaming red when frost time approaches. The sea milkwort, gentle little cousin of the primrose family, has tiny purple-pink blossoms. Most conspicuous of all is the marsh rosemary. This is a perennial with a group of long, rather heavy leaves growing from the crown. From June to mid-September the stems hold erect bouquets of interlaced sprays.

The highest zone of all in the salt marshes is the narrow rim near the mainland to which the tides seldom sweep. Once in a while in fall and spring at the full of the moon, when the great

119

semiannual surgings are helped by a northeaster, the salt water comes to the region of the black grass. Many people never realize the existence of this zone, for it averages only a few yards in width—sometimes only a few feet. Blackjack belongs to the rush family, for it has a rounded stem, and when the plant blossoms, the small purplish-black flowers make little dark islands of color on the greenish-brown carpet.

Here, in the blackjack belt, one can find that most gorgeous of the goldenrods—the seaside goldenrod. And in some spots the feathery-headed, golden-tan sweet-grass blossoms are mixed in friendly fashion with the goldenrod and blackjack.

August is perhaps the high twelve of the year in the spreading, quiet marshes. The marsh hawk coasts slowly along the air currents; savanna sparrows call from the drumlins; at sunrise and sunset the bittern's hollow "stake driving" rolls from a slough.

Few people know the beauty of the marshes; few take the time and trouble to explore their varied and distinct seasons of floral life. But anyone who loves the flavor of the sea knows they have much to offer.

Birches in the Dunes

✿ ✿

WHERE THE WINDS and waves have joined forces to throw up sand dunes between ocean and the good soil that supports crops or timberland, one of the poignant pictures is a clump of gray birches slowly surrendering to the forces that inexorably build and rebuild the sands. Man cannot understand all the secrets of Nature, for Nature holds within herself the secret of life. But anyone who is sensitive to secrets revealed can know the story of the dying birches.

Years ago a seed came floating through the air. The breeze that carried it scattered thousands of other seeds on the sand. But at this particular spot there was a bit of soil; the seed was covered at just the right depth. There followed days when atmospheric conditions of sun, clouds, and moisture were favorable. The miracle of life took place, and a little green shoot started upward. Over the years the struggle never ceased, but season after season the gray birch sent its roots farther and spread its branches wider. After a decade the humble slender-branched tree seemed firmly established in the sand. Its mottled gray bark with soot-colored streaks and the fragile, pendulant branches made an appealing picture against the background of the dunes. Then came a series of great storms in winter. The loose sand ran in swirling waves before the tempest. It began to pile around the stem of the tree. The little heap grew larger, and a windrow of sand climbed high against the trunk. Storm followed storm, and the time of the gray birch was fulfilled.

One sees the dying birches frequently in the dunes. Gallantly they fight. Each summer green leaves wave in the balmy air; but year by year the dead limbs increase and the number of leaves grows fewer. The birches stand like dry-point etchings in the expanse of sands—reminders of the never-ceasing battles of the dunes.

David W. Corson: A. Devaney, Inc., New York

Leaping Surf

✿ ✿

THE OCEAN is ever restless. Even on peaceful days in the heart of summer when the water's surface is placid and the tides switch calmly back and forth, there are rocky places along the meeting line between land and sea where geysers of water spring like living things into sunny air. In a great gale the leaping surf puts on its most dramatic act. During the awful fury of a winter's storm, when high waves crash against jagged cliffs, the spume flies high and sweeps far shoreward on the shoulders of a northeaster.

There is another type of leaping surf that is beautiful to watch and to study. On a summer day when the rollers are a few feet high, when the tide is making, and when a moderate wind is blowing landward, the rhythmically paced waves hit the rocks and throw green-white towers of lace into the air. The sun shines through the foamy spires. Beautiful symphonies of color poise for a few seconds before the shattered columns drop into the seething mass at the bases of the rocks.

Around the rocks is an eternal surging battle. As the waves come in and as they withdraw, the green-gray water is twisting, turning, attacking, and counterattacking. Curlicues of cream-white froth move restlessly on the surface. Foamy patterns are woven of watery strings and then are quickly ripped to pieces. Then a new wave moves in with its crested plume catching the sunlight. Sparkling gleams of red, orange, and russet twinkle for a moment. The wave hits the rock, and a white tower of water reaches into the air. The marshes and dunes and headlands drowse beneath the sun. Twice each day, when the waters surge toward the land, the leaping surf adds beauty along the shore line.

Marsh Wren

∗ ∗

THE MARSH WREN is a tiny singing troubadour by the edge of the sea. One of his favorite haunts is along the borders of spreading marshes where the thatch grass grows thick and tall. He likes the swampy area just above the black mud lines of sluggish rivers where the tide ripples through the reeds twice a day. Sometimes there are brackish swamps just above the reach of the tide, and here, where the sturdy-stemmed cattails make patterns of exclamation points, *Telmatodytes palustris* stakes out a homestead.

The long-billed marsh wren, to give him his full name, has a flair and stylishness that set him apart from his humble relative, the house wren. The latter clings to the farmsteads and dooryards; the marsh wren is a blithe spirit of the lonely stretches by the sea. His ½-inch bill, his jerky, stubby tail that seems to curve toward his back, the rakish white line over his eye, the black-and-white stripes on his upper body, and his beady black eyes combine to give *Telmatodytes* a fashion-page appearance.

He has his peculiarities and idiosyncrasies. While his dun-colored mate attends to household duties, he proceeds to build a half dozen or more nests attached to strong reeds or cattails. None of the handsome umber-brown eggs will be laid in any of these; the head of the family simply builds extra nests as a hobby to work off some of his excess energy.

The song of the long-billed marsh wren is part of the music along the land's edge. It does not have the melody of the warblers or the sweet poignancy of the thrushes, but what the longbill lacks in technique and quality, he compensates for by sheer buoyancy of spirit. Through the long days of spring and summer one can hear his joyous operatic trills sounding from marshy spots. He chooses isolated locations for his home, but it is well worth the effort to get close enough to hear his cheerful song.

Ghost Crab

✿ ✿

OCYPODE ARENARIA lives up to his popular name of ghost crab because the casual visitor to the dunes and upper beach is unlikely to see him. He is the only sizable crustacean along the northern coast that has left the water to live entirely on land.

Sitting quietly at the base of a dune crest or on the dry stretch above the high-tide line some summer day, one may notice numerous small circular burrows, each with small piles of sand beside it. With his eyes fastened on one of the burrows, he may see, after the commotion of his arrival has passed, one of the most peculiar creatures of the shore line. Perhaps dozens of the ghost crabs have been crouching quietly near him, their pale sand-colored bodies blending with the environment.

If all is quiet the crab lifts one eyestalk slowly. Presently the other comes erect. Slowly the little beast rises on its legs and begins a peculiar side-winding walk. Suddenly it rises to the full height of its shell-jointed legs, as if standing on tiptoe. If danger seems to threaten, the crab flattens out and remains motionless on the sand. If one attempts to corner *Ocypode arenaria*, he will learn that the ghost crab is fleet and nimble, adept at dodging, and clever with his camouflaging act.

Watching a ghost crab emerge from its burrow is an interesting experience. First come the two front legs. Then the tip of one or both eyestalks comes into view. For a full minute or more there is no further movement. Then, satisfied with its careful reconnaissance, the crab emerges, clasping a load of sand against its body with one claw and two or three forelegs. It tosses the sand away and darts back to the burrow opening, takes another long survey, and then disappears for a second load. Around the mouth of its tunnel home the crab builds a circular rim of sand. When danger threatens, it pulls the sand inward and seals the mouth of the burrow.

The ghost crab lives on bits of seaweed, sand hoppers, beetles,

125

and other insects. He stalks his prey like a jungle animal, inching forward slowly and cautiously. Then he gathers his legs beneath him and leaps forward to capture his victim. Like the other branches of the numerous crab family, he prefers live food, but he is not at all fastidious. After a picnic party has left the beach, the ghost crabs congregate and feast on the debris that too often remains behind.

Adapted in color to their sandy environment, timid and fearful, the small ghost crabs scuttle hesitatingly about between periods of watching. Instinctive caution governs their every movement. They are a part of the often unnoticed life on the upper sands.

Thatch Grass

☼ ☼

THERE IS a certain haunting appeal about the salt marshes when the ninth month rolls around. Up and down the coast line one senses the mood of September. There are broad expanses of the flat land to which the tide comes only once or twice each month at the full of the moon; there are small curving marshes that nestle against the mainland. Here and there one sees the drumlins, low-lying earth-islands of glacial deposit left years ago when the last ice era ended.

The thatch grass is a marker of the tides; for unless the soil is covered twice daily with salt water, the tall, reedy grass ceases to grow. This fact contributes to Nature's constantly changing pattern along the shore. Thatch grass grows thickly; the tides bring in more and more silt and sand. The thatch claims this soil-building material, and day by day, month by month, and year by year, the soil line creeps higher. For months and years the thatch grass holds its own by sending out roots higher and higher from its hollow stem. But Nature is inexorable; one area is built up as another is torn down. When the thatch grass has built up the earth high enough so that the ocean does not wash it twice a day, the grass dies, and then the marsh hay—the fox, sea spear, and spike grasses—claims the region.

September is a good time to study the thatch. It makes a fringe along the lines of high tide just at the edge of the ocean's reach. It makes circles around the drumlins and borders the muddy marsh creeks where the tides ebb and flow. The golden-tan plumes of seed branches, like ripe oats, wave gently in the mellow ninth-month sun. The tall, slender reeds are just one of the many plants of the marshes, but their stately beauty contributes much to the whole quiet picture.

Whittling Lobster Pegs

* *

FROM THE TIME in early spring when the climbing sun circles closer to the pole of the horizon until after the period of the autumnal equinox the whittlers can be seen sitting in the open doorways of weather-silvered fishhouses. Seated on old boxes and crates tipped back against the sides of the picturesque shanties, they methodically shape slender lobster pegs.

Sometimes there is a group of elderly men in a sunny nook of a granite-walled wharf, whittling and reminiscing together. For half a century they have gone down to the sea for a living. Some of them have tended strings of lobster pots along the hard-bottomed shelf of the shore line; others have known the dangers and hardships of the Grand Banks in the days when men fished by hand lines and trawls from dories. Their faces are lined; their hands are rough and gnarled. Now in the sunset years they whittle lobster pegs for younger men who go out at dawn for the big-clawed macrural crustaceans.

There's nothing complicated about the task of whittling. It's a job for elderly fishermen who want to earn a few dollars a week and who want to keep busy. To anyone who knows the life in snug harbors along the coast, it suggests more than the actual work of making tangy-smelling shavings curl away from sharp knives. A line of small fishhouses in the sun, a conglomeration of weathered lobster pots, colorful buoys, discarded boat gear, and unhurried philosophical men who are enjoying the peaceful years complete a picture of life by the sea. Whittling lobster pegs is a utilitarian job that serves a purpose.

Sunrise over the Waters

✿ ✿

IN THE VAST, unmeasured space we label the universe the planet Earth spins on her axis and takes her route around the sun. Each day Earth turns her back for a few hours on the Giver of Light; each day she welcomes the dawn. Fortunate is he who knows the pristine beauty of the day's birth when the sun seems to climb from beneath the waters of the eastern horizon.

Each of the year's major seasons offers its own peculiar and distinctive loveliness. Winter's cold dawning reflects brilliant white diamonds from the ruffled wave tips above sullen steel-gray waters. On a cloudless day in the time of deep cold the sun rises late and reluctantly and starts its low course across the southern sky. The slanting rays pick up jewel-like gleams from the ice-coated rocks along the craggy headlands. As the light strikes the frosted grasses of the marshes, there's a short period when the level stretches between ocean and mainland are a fairyland of breath-taking enchantment. Each stalk of thatch grass, blackjack, and marsh goldenrod is a stem of twinkling beauty. The ice-crusted meandering windrows of grass and kelp on the beaches are long necklaces of mixed jewels, sparkling with shades of red, blue, orange, and green. Winter's sunrise over the waters is beautiful, but lovely, cold, and sear. It comes slowly, in tune with the faint pulse of the season.

In May the coming of dawn is a different story. For an hour before the first circular tip of the sun shows above the spot where waves meet the sky, there's a spreading screen of lightness in the East. Before the sun shows, the bird symphony begins. In the thickets of the drumlins, in the tangled growth of sumacs, locusts, and bayberries along the shore, among the dunes and over the marshes, the song sparrows, robins, and wood pewees throw their hearts to the sky, welcoming day's return. Just as the sun lifts into view, if atmospheric conditions are right, there is a period of flaming beauty that rivals, on a miniature scale, the glory of a summer sunset. Long streaks of saffron,

130

gold, and russet red shoot upward to the zenith—a fanfare to welcome spring dawn.

Perhaps a majority of those who love the sea and the message that it brings to man's spirit would choose a summer day's sunrise. It is the time of quietness when Nature's fulfillment is near. The ocean drowses, its restlessness partially stilled for a time. Hushed now is the dawn symphony of the birds. Light comes softly to the sky in the East. The curtain of night lifts silently along the shore and over the waters. From coves and harbors men set out quietly in their boats to tend their lobster pots. Minute by minute more light drops on the land and sea. The flashing gleam of a lighthouse suddenly ceases. Small sheets of waves tentatively feel their way up the beach, hesitate a moment, and break apart in lace-curtain patterns as they roll back on the firm bed of sand. The start of the incoming tide plays a game with the swinging, graceful eelgrass in the mouths of marsh creeks. Little ponds of mist blossom briefly in the hollows among the dunes and then disappear as the climbing sun's rays strike into the low spots. On the tops of the dunes patches of brown-green beach grass are silhouetted against the sky. Even before the sun has climbed free of the water, a marsh hawk may start its soaring, or perhaps a great blue heron may come to a creek and then stand motionless, a statue in the growing light. Blue-gray smoke curls up from chimneys of houses on the hillsides above the harbors. The night herons wing their way homeward to the red pine groves. Free of the ocean, the sun climbs swiftly. Suddenly a flock of sandpipers begins teetering and bobbing along the beach; a group of herring gulls starts screaming. Summer dawn surrenders to summer day.

When summer's time is ended and October slides downhill toward November, there comes still another type of sunrise. It does not have the cold ominousness of winter, but when one watches light come to a day of the eleventh month, he can sense the drawing of the curtain on the third act of the drama. The ocean and the land are waiting for winter. There is a flickering of frozen spume on the rocks. The sand on the beaches is broken into tiny caverns and abysses, and tiny flecks of ice crunch underfoot. As darkness lifts from the muted world, gray splotches appear in the eastern sky, the advance scouts of the sun. All earth and sky and water wear a gray cloak. The sun pulls up and starts its course. There's a chilly sense of season's end. Lonely are the beaches, dunes, and marshes. In the cold dawn light they lie starkly revealed. Sunrise in November is a part of the ocean's mood. Earth's breast grows hard as she prepares for her long sleep. The gray dawn light of late autumn is a prelude to the winter ocean's crashing symphony.

Sumacs by the Shore

THE STAGHORN SUMAC is one of the appealing small trees along the coast line. From Nova Scotia to Georgia it lifts its irregular branches above the thin-soiled earth along craggy coasts; it stands like a precisely engraved steel etching on the dunes—a bit of Oriental art against a tan-brown background. On glacial drumlins that dot wide-spreading marshes the sumacs make underbrush beneath locusts, birches, and scrub oaks. At the rear of marshes where the tide-washed flats meet the soil of the mainland, there are often belts of the sumacs that mark the armistice line between ocean and good soil.

Rhus hirta is a distinctive fellow. It is often called velvet sumac because of the year-round dense growth of velvety hairs on the backs of young branches. Through the summer the long, pointed, shallowly serrated leaves make a background for the developing cones of berries that form from the dense panicles of green-yellow blossoms. Along the coast, though the soil be stony and infertile, the enlarging cones tell a story of Nature's plan. Fogs from the ocean roll in and bathe the long leaves and moisten the land. Week by week the cones with their fuzz-covered berries undergo a series of color transformations. They change from a light yellowish tan to a pink; then to henna, to rich brown, and eventually to the deep maroon that holds its color far into the winter.

November is a good time to see the red pennants on the sumacs. On the headlands, on the granite-based peninsulas, and along the fringes of woods where trees march down to the ocean, the sumacs stand through the brown days with their pointed pennants. Later the winter birds come for the nutlets inside the fuzz coverings; white-tailed deer wander into the thickets and nibble the cones. Sumacs may grow to a height of 30 feet; more commonly they are 12 to 20 feet. They're not important trees, but they're familiar ones to those who are sensitive to the flavor of the coast line.

133

Timbers in the Sands

❖ ❖

HERE AND THERE along the coast timbers can be seen in the sands—stark, blackened timbers partially exposed to summer's brooding heat and winter's buffeting gales. They crouch half hidden on upper beaches near the ramparts of the dunes; they lie forlornly isolated on sand arms that reach out into the sea. Occasionally one sees a bit of lichen-covered framework resting on a stretch of rocky shore line or wedged tightly in a cliff-walled canyon that gashes into the mainland.

The timbers in the sands tell a poignant story. Depending on the power of wind and tide, they show or hide their skeletons. Sometimes the high tides of spring and fall will pull the sand away, and through the summer and into the fall the gray-black symmetrically spaced ribs make a broken silhouette against the white sands. Or perhaps a familiar landmark along the shore suddenly disappears, covered for a time by the comminuted particles ground fine by the millstones of the sea.

Long years ago these scarred, weathered ribs were part of a proud ship. Before it slid down splintery ways into a high tide, skilled craftsmen swung their short-handled adzes to carve the proud swell of the vessel's bosom. Planks were fitted tightly with long, tapering oaken pegs. Decks were made firm, and a solid superstructure was built. For an unknown time the vessel plowed a furrow in the water and served the needs of man. Then came the end. Perhaps bells tolled from a white-spired church in a little fishing village. The sea had claimed another offering. Long years ago it happened. Now the last of the ship lifts silent, patient fingers. The gaunt, quiet timbers in the sands are a memorial to men and vessels of the past.

135

Fishing Villages in Autumn

✵ ✵

As THE YEAR rolls into the brown month, one can almost feel that time is running downhill to low twelve. There's a slowing of tempo in the little clustered fishing villages above small harbors, coves, and inlets. Days seem but brief interludes between periods of darkness. There's a brown-gray sheen to the ocean and the water looks cold and forbidding. There are long periods of cloudy weather when the moisture-laden clouds seem held as if by a magnet close above land and ocean. Occasionally there are days of peculiarly brilliant sunshine. The sun rises like a great ball of red fire, and for a few brief hours all the shore line, the village, and the boats in the harbor are etched in sharp, clear detail.

Whether cloudy weather or bright, the fisherfolk go about their work in unhurried calmness. Lobstermen pull methodically on the oars as they go from pot to pot; old men with grizzled faces and eyes that have looked far over restless waters sit around the rusty stoves in their weather-beaten shanties and mend nets, paint buoys, and whittle lobster pegs.

As day draws to a close and night's curtain drops on ocean and land, lights begin to gleam above the shore. The village is an upland field dotted with yellow daisies against a blue-black background. The street lights make spots of golden glow in the darkness. Lights gleam in lonely warning from buoys in the harbor, and far across the bay is the intermittent flash of a lighthouse. Darkness deepens; lights go out in the fishing shanties; men climb the streets to homes that nestle against the hillside. Day draws to a close in a little fishing village in autumn.

Salt Marsh in October

THERE COMES A TIME in autumn when the marshes have a poignant appeal for one who delights in savoring the flavor of the sea. The salt marshes are an integral part of the environment in the area that the ocean dominates. Twice a day the sea gathers its strength and sends its waves rolling landward. The salt marsh depends upon the ocean. The thatch grass and blackjack reeds need salt water twice daily; on the higher stretches the fox grass and spike grass must have it twice a month, when the position of the full moon and first-quarter moon ordain the high lunar tides.

In October there is beauty on the marshes. Frost has seared the grasses, and a brown blanket stretches over the area. There's a brooding, peaceful spirit on the flat landscape. Great white clouds wander across the blue, blue sky; tall blue herons stand like carved statues. White gulls wing through the air; marsh hawks circle slowly overhead. Wide bands of sea goldenrod form bright necklaces against the tan-brown grass. October's brilliant sun lights the paths of the twisting creeks at high tide; they seem, for a brief interlude, like silvery-blue ribbons tying the grassy stretches together.

On the drumlins, low-wooded islands of the marshes, the oaks, locusts, birches, and sumacs make the rounded hills look like great bouquets of reds and yellows and browns. Over all the expanse is that soft purplish haze that Nature spreads when the year's clock begins to slow down. For an interlude there's peace and loveliness before the harsh hand of King Winter flings desolation abroad over the landscape.

Teetertail

✿ ✿

THE FRIENDLY, individualistic little spotted sandpiper sets a good example of democratic processes in a world where relationships are somewhat harried and tangled. Teetertail subscribes to the philosophy that so long as he doesn't bother others, he expects reciprocal consideration. Not that he's unduly aloof or self-centered. His folklore names—tiptail, tiltup, and teeter—are evidences of the fact that he observes the amenities. After he has been startled into a low, short flight, he circles back to where he took off and then proceeds to bow to the four points of the compass. He's likely to make obeisance with his head, then turn around and bob his sawed-off tail.

He's a distinctive-looking fellow in spite of his primness. His back is olive-ash color, and his underbody is peppered with a helter-skelter pattern of large and small, round, sooty dots. There is a rakish white bar over his eye. His long bill is a tannish-pink hue. When he is running along the wet beach as the tide is waning, he keeps his head down. Every once in a while he stops and probes an area in systematic, industrious fashion. When spring is deepening toward summer, his demure mate sits on four or five tan-colored eggs heavily spotted with rusty black at the large ends. The nest is well hidden in a thick clump of brownish-green beach grass.

Tiptail doesn't assume many family responsibilities; he leaves the domestic side of affairs to his competent, uncomplaining mate. But one of his many names, sand lark, tells its own story. Periodically, he soars upward above the dunes and takes a long wheel over the marsh between the sand and mainland. As he flies he sends forth his trilling, happy song, "Peet-t-tweet, peet-t-tweet." He is only a common little spotted sandpiper, but the beach and dunes would be lonely without him.

138

Least Terns

✿ ✿

STERNA ANTILLARUM ANTILLARUM is an imposing, rolling nomenclature for such a small bird of the ocean's fringe. The least tern is generally regarded as the most dainty as well as one of the smallest of the sea birds. Rarely over 9 inches in length and with a wingspread of only 20 inches, little striker, as he is frequently called, is a part of the flavor of the sea from Massachusetts southward. He's a handsome chap in his pure white cape, shiny black cap, white patch on his forehead, and black-tipped golden-yellow bill.

The least terns prefer the open beaches and the barren land arms, which are fully exposed to the ocean's moods. Sometimes they choose nesting sites where very high tides wash completely over a sand spit. Here, in the open sand, the females hollow out nests and each broods her two or three tannish-brown eggs. The least terns are gregarious and sociable; many families seem to operate in clans. On occasion, when a marsh hawk comes sailing along, unhurriedly and low, a group of enraged terns attack with startling ferocity. Ordinarily they cheep at the world in a rather plaintive, complaining way, but when danger threatens, they scream and bluster in shrill, raspy voices that remind one of herring gulls fighting over a fish.

The least tern has one appealing trait. After the young are hatched, the male comes circling in with sweet, thin calls and lights beside the nest. After he has fed the little ones, he stands beside them to furnish shade while his mate flies away to do a bit of food hunting for herself. As the terns course above the water and then suddenly dive into the blue-green rolling waves, they remind one of black-dotted snowflakes dropping into the ocean. The flavor of the sea would not be complete without their friendly presence.

Kosti Ruohomaa: Black Star

Winter Ocean

✿ ✿

VIEWED FROM a rocky promontory that juts into the sea, where the jagged, tumbled granite boulders reach to the water line at low tide, whether bright day or gray, the mood of the ocean in the last month is predominantly the same. That mood tells man of the unfathomable power of the sea. On a calm, sunny day, as the thin rays of light pierce the foam caps and reflect white jewels from the gray, roiled waters between the waves, one can sense the restless, stirring strength of the cold ocean.

On a gray day when the nimbus clouds are swelling and the wind is rising, the waves writhe and hiss about the rocks at one's feet. The moss-lined tidal pools among the higher rocks are miniature ponds, sheeted with gray ice and decorated with lacy patterns of frozen spume. Out on the ocean lanes an occasional ship plods steadily toward its destination, the black smoke drifting like a slender cloud to the south and southeast. Minute by minute one can feel the power of the storm increase and hear the answering roar from the excited ocean.

It is an exhilarating experience to stand for a time on the rocks in the midst of a great winter storm. All the mighty power of the sea is marshaled into a climactic effort. The gray-green waves hurdle the low-lying rocky ramparts and spring in fury at a higher goal. The water leaps into the air, and tangents of froth and bubbly foam make a wild picture to accompany the hoarse bellows when the main part of the waves is dashed into frustrated rage. The winter ocean can erupt in volcanic fury; the strength that was held in reserve through the calm of summer and early fall is exploded against land and marsh, piers and beach. Anyone who thrills to the power of natural elements feels his soul lift to the majesty of the ocean's power in the heart of winter.

Sanderlings

❋ ❋

THE SANDERLINGS are true followers of the sea. After the waves have rolled onto the beaches, hesitated, and spread into thin plastic-looking sheets edged with innumerable ruffles of white air-foam, the little bull peeps run over the wet, smooth-packed sand garnering a harvest of worms, small crustaceans, and mollusks.

Their dusty-black legs and long, pointed toes twinkle back and forth as they scurry along, watching for the foods washed ashore by the turmoil of the sea. They know that the incoming tide brings windrow after windrow of tiny morsels of food and deposits them momentarily on the sloping sands. The backwash may claim a part of the harvest but some of it will remain. The alert, industrious little fellows follow the receding water; sometimes they even run into shallow, retiring waves to snatch morsels.

As the tide turns and a wave begins its rolling progress landward, the peepers scamper nimbly up the wet sand just ahead of it. Occasionally they run too far into the gray-green water, and the oncoming wave forces them to rise with a burst of beating wings and circle back to the beach. Sometimes on a quiet summer day at dead low tide a sizable flock will suddenly lift from the beach and fly low along the shore line to a mud flat at the mouth of a marsh creek. Here it may spend half an hour or more poking around the muddy area in a lackadaisical manner.

Crocethia alba is a small bird of 7 or 8 inches in length. He is larger than the spotted sandpiper and has a wingspread of 15 or 16 inches. In the spring when he first returns from the South he wears a brown cape over his back. Toward the end of summer the brown begins to disappear, and by mid-September his upper body is a mottled cloak of shades of dark gray. When the sanderlings are in flight, they show white bars in the centers of their wings, making bold contrasts to the black of

142

their other flight feathers. Their beady black eyes are surrounded by circles of white. Shoremen and fishermen, clam diggers and lobstermen have given *Crocethia* a roster of nicknames—beach bird, whitey (in the fall he's the whitest of all shore birds), whiting, stib, white snipe, and beach snipe.

These "peepers of the sand" have little fear of people. On hot days when groups of human beings are enjoying the ocean's edge, flocks of sanderlings run up and down, back and forth, within a score of yards of them. As they poke the hard, wet sands, they put on an interesting show. While the semipalmated sandpiper runs around in aimless, haphazard fashion, probing briefly in one spot and then rushing to another a few yards away, the sanderling goes at it in a more organized fashion. He suddenly decides that a certain spot offers possibilities and seemingly forgets the rest of the small flock with which he customarily travels. While the other birds trot on to another location, he energetically begins what one might call his "plowing." In reality it is a rapid series of downward thrusts of his powerful bill. He proceeds in an almost straight line or a gently curving one. The probings are very close together, and when he is satisfied, or perhaps dissatisfied, with the returns of the spot, they resemble a miniature furrow plowed in the wet sand. As he walks forward in search of sand fleas and tiny crustaceans, rapidly plunging his bill into the sand and lifting his head in preparation for another downward stroke, he always throws the sand in advance. The procedure might remind one of a tiny V-shaped snowplow, as the shower of sand flies in either direction from his bill.

His mate is somewhat casual about her choice of a nesting site. Sometimes she selects a partly hidden spot beneath a clump of beach grass or a sheltered nook in a tangle of dried seaweed, kelp, and debris on the upper rim of the beach. The home is a slight hollow in the sand, often carelessly lined with grass and bits of leaves. The three or four eggs are most interesting; they are pear shaped, olive-brown, and peppered with tiny flecks of dark, ruddy brown.

The sanderlings make their contribution to the ever-changing picture by the sea. Their staccato "cheep, cheep" is a running commentary on their activities. Rarely are they quiet. Their slender legs work like rhythmic pistons as they hurry toward the water and then bustle landward to keep ahead of an oncoming wave. Bull peep isn't an extrovert like the gull, but he is an integral part of life along the ocean's edge.

Barnacles

❀ ❀

IN THE MIDST of seemingly prosaic surroundings anyone who is sensitive to the mysteries of Nature's workings discovers many unusual forms of life. Countless human beings walk along the rocky coast line and tread on myriad tiny, gray-colored shells without knowing the interesting life story of the shore barnacle. Cirripedia resembles a miniature volcano. He is a crustacean, cousin to the shrimp, crab, and lobster.

In its first stage, after hatching from a tiny, black egg, the young barnacle swims about in the water along the shore. After it changes its shell several times, it becomes attached to its permanent home and develops its hard outer covering of six or eight sections. The opening at the top enables the slender feather-like legs to wave about in the water when the tide is high and to push bits of food within reach. As the feeders wave back and forth, the hinged sections of the wall are pushed apart to give the legs more freedom of movement. When the water recedes, the feeders are pulled in, the sections of the shell are tightly closed, and the barnacle rests until the ocean sends its waters surging landward again.

The goose barnacles, the large cream-colored shell types that attach themselves in tremendous numbers to the bottoms of ships and that grow in bunches on the rocks just above the line of low tide, have an interesting bit of folklore connected with them. Their long legs resemble the necks of geese, and their large shells look a bit like geese's eggs. In centuries past men actually believed they were the eggs of some phantom goose.

If one listens carefully as he walks along the rocks where the tidal pools have just been replenished and the tide is going out, he will hear, as he comes upon a section where thousands of the tiny barnacles pepper the gray rocks, a faint whisper, like a wandering breeze among the grasses of a marsh. That gentle, breathlike whisper is the closing of the shells as the barnacles withdraw into themselves to wait for another time of high water.

145

David W. Corson: A. Devaney, Inc., New York

Old Shipyards

✿ ✿

UP AND DOWN the coast line one finds many old shipyards—in sheltered coves and harbors, at the backs of marshes where the tides are high enough for launching, along the banks of saltwater rivers that have ebb and flow, and in rocky-armed nooks by the ocean's edge.

For more than two centuries some of the yards have echoed to the hollow, reverberating thumps of wooden mallets and the chip-chips of wide-bladed adzes. They are labyrinthine jungles of boats in process of construction, stacked piles of planking, heaps of short, thick timbers for ships' ribs, and jackstraw tangles of miscellaneous boards and dimension stuff. Frequently, at one side there are half a dozen or more long timbers earmarked as keels of future ships. Old, weather-beaten sheds and shanties at the upper edge of the yard house tools and equipment. A power saw in a sprawling low building now does much of the work that pioneer craftsmen once did by hand.

The shipyard is littered with bark, small pieces of wood, and the chippings from the adzes. The air is filled with a heavy, pungent fragrance compounded of sawdust, drying bark, old wood, and freshly peeled logs. Over all is the invigorating smell of the sea. When the tide is out and the wind is shoreward, the tangy odor of the mud and marsh is the dominant note. When the tide is making and the water ripples at the end of the launching ways, there's another fragrance—not the pungent aroma of mud exposed to the sun, but a lighter, spicier smell that one gets only in an old, old shipyard on a sparkling summer day.

The picturesque yards along the coast still serve man's needs. They are a link with the long-ago days when pioneers made their first new homes close to the sea and began to build ships to gather some of the ocean's harvest.

Seaside Goldenrod

❁ ❁

THERE ARE more than fifty species of goldenrod in North America. When summer draws on toward fall, the first copper-gold tints of *Solidago sempervirens,* the seaside goldenrod, begin to knit mufflers around the necks of marshes where they fit into the mainland. The book of words is terse with its definition: "Any of a genus (*Solidago*) or of several related genera of summer-blooming and fall-blooming carduaceous perennials or biennials with wandlike stems, variously shaped leaves, and heads of small yellow, or rarely white, flowers, often clustered in panicles. Species have been adopted as State flowers by Alabama, Kentucky, and Nebraska."

The salt-tolerant species is perhaps the loveliest of all the goldenrods. It makes its tallest growth, with peculiarly glossy, dark-green foliage and handsome large flowers, around the marsh fringes, but one can often find it in the little hollows among the dunes where thickets of bayberries and gray birches make sanctuary for wildlife. In September and October before killing frosts blight foliage, the golden plumes wave in the breezes that ruffle the tall thatch grass by mud creeks and send ripples through the shorter grasses in the flat marshlands. Their islands of color in the dunes, the long, narrow bands that make a lace along the marshes in the fall, are part of the beauty near the sea.

When one walks on the marshes in midwinter and the land is powdered with snow and rime, there's a poignant beauty in the gray-bleached plumes on sturdy stalks that stand like gallant banners above the winter-blighted land. They remind one of beauty past and beauty still to come in the fullness of time.

Marsh Hay

✵ ✵

MANY A FARM, though a few miles inland, has in its ancient
deed a right of way to the salt marshes and a few acres there
for haying if the farmer wishes. Time was, a generation ago,
when marsh hay was important. There are still many places along
the coast where men go out in August to harvest it. The marsh-
hay area is the third zone of vegetation from the sea—above the
eelgrass at the creeks' mouths and above the spreading areas
of thatch grass. Only a few times a year do the surging tides
roll up over the level stretches where the fox, sea spear, and
spike grasses, which combine to make marsh hay, grow.

In years past, horses with big wooden shoes pulled the mowing machines over the drier areas; men with rhythmic motion
swung snaths and scythes in the sloughs and wet spots. Sometimes there were marsh islands surrounded by mud creeks, and
the hay was rowed across on flat barges at high tide. When the
wiry grasses were cured, the hay was stacked on staddles—
groups of oak or cedar posts driven into the soft soil and ex-
tending a foot or so above the surface. In the winter when the
upper marsh was frozen hard, farmers would come with oxen
and horses and haul home great loads. It was used mostly for
bedding, but if it were cut in late July or early August, it had
nourishment enough to winter the dry cows and neat stock.

Now along the coast line in certain sections farmers are harvesting the grasses. Long years ago the pioneers settled near
the sea's edge and used the marsh hay. Part of the history of
the making of this nation is linked to this seasonal task, for as
men and women made homes along the ocean and then pushed
frontiers from the Atlantic to the Pacific, they used Nature's
gifts from both the sea and the land.

149

Southward Flight

✿ ✿

WHEN SEPTEMBER'S HESITANCY gives way to October's burst of glory, the shoreman knows that the southward flight is on the way. Nature flings out her standards to proclaim the season. The sumacs lift maroon pennants; the seaside goldenrod holds its deep yellow banners stiffly erect. For a brief interlude after the first frost the spreading marshes are blankets of deep brown. The birches in the dunes are bouquets of gold, and the scrub oaks on the drumlins are Oriental rugs of scarlet, chestnut, yellow, and bronze.

The southward flight begins slowly. First, only members of the vanguard arrive. Some of them pause in their trek and rest a bit on the dunes and beaches. Then, as the month draws on and the tentative chills give way to killing frosts, the great migration arrives. Through thousands of years the birds have followed this trail along the edge of the ocean. In small flocks and large they drive southward to winter quarters, guided by an instinct man has not yet fathomed.

Anyone who is sensitive to Nature's deep messages can stand on the dunes in the dim light of the hunter's moon and capture some of the spirit of the seasonal mystery. Many of the birds travel by night and rest by day. They flash across the face of the moon like successive dots of gray. Their voices come down to earth, thin, lonesome, and wild. A period of Nature's cycle has ended. Cold is creeping down from the north. The southward flight has passed. Another chapter is finished.

November by the Ocean

❁ ❁

BROWN NOVEMBER, men label the eleventh month, and along the ocean's edge there is brownness where water and land meet. There is a brown-gray tinge to the sands of the beaches beneath low-lying, thick stratus clouds; brown seaweed lies in curving windrows where high tide has dropped its harvest. The cold-looking waves of the ocean have a brown-green hue as sunless days follow one another downhill toward low twelve of the year.

The dunes are solitary, lonesome places. The waves of driven sand stretch back from the sea in cold desolation. Gone now are the night herons and smaller birds from the islands of red pines in the dune valleys. The clumps of gray birches are etched against the sands like sharply limned steel engravings. Patches of tangled bayberries are heavy with their thick clusters of waxy berries. Along the line where sand or marsh meets the mainland soil, conventions of staghorn sumac hold aloft their banners of wine-red berries.

Perhaps on the spreading marshes one best senses November's brownness and the spirit of the slow running down of the season's clock. Black frosts have seared the tall thatch grass along the creeks where tides finger into the marsh-hay flats. Over the broad expanses where men cut fox grass and spike grass a few short weeks ago and built the conical-topped stacks of hay, all is brown, quiet, and lonely. The drumlins that dot the marshes are islands of brown, covered with the scrubby pasture oaks that hold onto their leaves far into the winter.

There's a spirit of ominousness and a threat in November by the ocean. Now is the time of great storms, when an uneasy sea lifts its power and hurls waves onto the battleground between itself and the land. To those who love the place where land and water meet, November offers something indefinable. True, it is austere and chilly; but it is honest and unpretentious, too. Nature is ever changing, and to one whose spirit is attuned, there is beauty in all seasons of the year.

152

Great Blue Heron

❀ ❀

THERE ARE many forms of wildlife that have double qualifications. They not only fit particular environments of forest, field, swamp, or marsh, but they also have the power to suggest certain traits and characteristics. Anyone who has seen a doe and her half-grown fawn poised for flight in an open glade has a memory of one of Nature's loveliest pictures. A vixen lying at guard before her den on a rocky hillside with her pups playing around her is another. A mother skunk stalking phlegmatically across a farmyard at early evening with a single line of her offspring spaced behind her not only is a touching sight, but her casual progress implies complete confidence in her power to control any situation that may arise.

In the bird world there is no other creature that rivals the great blue heron in its ability to fit the environment or to create a mood. *Ardea herodias* is found over a vast area of the continent—along sluggish rivers and creeks, beside ponds and lakes. But in no place, perhaps, does he typify certain virtues or seem to match the surroundings as well as when he stands in a shallow mud creek of the great marshes that lie between the ocean and the mainland. He is a solitary and lonely bird in the midst of widespread loveliness. He looks ponderous and slow. He has about him the spirit of primal days when grotesque forms of life inhabited steaming jungles and shores of inland seas.

For long periods the great bird is immobile. One senses the imperturbability and patience of Nature's hunter as he stands for minute after minute in the water, waiting—waiting—waiting. His long, slender neck is formed into an S; his big, bright yellow eyes with beady pupils concentrate without blinking on the water around his feet. Then suddenly, almost faster than human eye can follow, the powerful neck uncoils, the head darts downward; the beak goes into the water and comes up with a small fish or minnow. Then the patient, timeless stance is resumed.

It is an interesting experience to watch a heron walk along

153

in shallow water. He moves his seemingly ungainly, off-balance body with infinite poise and calm certainty. Each great foot with its four widespread claws is lifted very carefully and slowly; each foot in turn goes down again with care and control. And always those staring eyes are surveying the water with relentless intensity. Sometimes, as the great body moves evenly along, the head goes down and a fish is caught without breaking the effortless rhythm of the forward motion.

To the unthinking, the great blue heron is a mass of confused and top-heavy angles. But whether standing in infinite patience, stalking slowly along a creek, or soaring away in unhurried flight on his great wings, he is the personification of the power and patience of the great sea by whose shores he lives.

154

Marsh Creeks in Winter

✿ ✿

THERE IS a lonesome, poignant beauty in the marshes when the King of the Northland has turned his key and locked the land. Cold, barren, and desolate they seem to the casual eye, but the sensitive person, who would taste the flavor of the sea in all weathers, knows that behind the seeming bleakness is a story of interest. At the mouth of the muddy-banked inlets, where the tidewaters pass in and out twice a day, and along the twisting, steep-sided creeks that wind back through the flat marshes to the rim of the mainland, there are tales waiting to be read.

At dead low tide in the time of severe cold, the smallest creeks are roofed over with a sheet of blue-gray ice. As one stands in the knife-edged wind, he can hear cold water crackling back and forth, unseen beneath its covering. In the middle-sized creeks, from 8 to 12 feet wide, there are small, jagged pieces of ice lying beside the banks on the frayed blankets of brown frost-killed grass. Where the banks are slanting there's a pattern of ice pieces on the black mud—mud that is frozen into tortured crevices and miniature abysses. Along the large creeks, where the tides have a better chance to roll and swirl, the banks are buttresses of jagged ice. Large and small pieces are heaped together in haphazard fashion. In very cold weather sheets of green-gray, porous-looking ice form over the creeks. At high tide the sheets are lifted and ride suspended on the water at the level of the marsh grass; at low tide they sink down and rest on the mud until the ocean hurls its waves again at the shore line.

There is beauty in the marshes on gray or bright days in winter—lonesome, cold, and quiet beauty. Following along the creeks one sees ever-changing pictures of the awesome power of the sea. These heaps of ice cakes, the roofs over the creeks, the monotonous roaring of the waters that beat on the shores are all symbols of the battle between elemental forces.

Moonlight on the Ocean

✿ ✿

THERE ARE MANY who find solace and renewed strength in the spirit of the sea. They know the ocean's moods through the year's seasons. Human hearts respond to spring's increasing beauty, to summer's peaceful interlude, to autumn's gathering grayness, to winter's cold barrenness. Many would agree, however, that one of the ocean's most appealing and heart-stirring times of loveliness is that of a late-rising full moon lifting from the water and unrolling a shining path across the waves.

All is quiet on land and sea. Far hills are dim silhouettes against a blue-black skyline; marshes are broad meadows of gray. As the first circular bit of the moon appears, there is a soft gray apron of light that spreads from the pale green-yellow of the moon. Minute by minute the color of the moon deepens; minute by minute the pathway of light creeps across the dark water to the land. Then the moon lifts itself free of the horizon's edge and begins its climb.

The path from the moon to land's edge widens, and the soft gray turns to gleaming silver. As minutes flow by, the moon's rays weave a jeweled blanket on Ocean's loom. If the night is still and Heaven's meadow is abloom with red and orange and diamond-blue stars, one can see the shimmering reflections in the moon's silver streamer. Quarter hour by quarter hour the beauty intensifies. The wave-tops crochet lines of silvery lace; the rolling dunes become land waves of silver-gray sands. Lights from harbor buoys make golden dots above the water, and flashes from an island lighthouse make staccato hyphens on night's dark page. Over the brooding sea the moon sails serenely among the stars.

Winter Beach

✿ ✿

How SHOULD ONE describe the beach in the heart of winter? On a gray, quiet day in January there is about it a sense of ominous foreboding. Thick, soot-streaked nimbus clouds hang low over the gray-black waters of the sea. They are close above the gray-brown sand of the beach; they make a dark gray monotone of the dunes and turn the tan of the wide-spreading marshes to a lifeless shade halfway between gray and brown.

There are few places on earth where one so quickly senses the moods of an ever-changing Nature as on the strip of land that is subject to the tides. In the depth of winter the predominant mood is one of tenseness and waiting. There are, of course, some days of brilliant sunshine when the slanting rays of the sun pick up glints in the whitetops that break over the crests of rollers. For a few fleeting seconds the cold, green-streaked waves shake a frothy white plume in the sun's face. One can see far up and down the coast in the peculiar intensity of the pale winter sunlight. Lighthouses and hilltops miles away are silhouetted against the steel-blue sky. The clumps of brown beach grass on the dune crests are etched in stark detail. The windrows of icy, bubbly spume on the beach mark the lines of high tide. For a brief time at high noon the ocean and the land beside it are starkly illumined in a pitiless, glaring light.

But the predominant color is gray. Frequently, after a morning of sunlight, the clouds gather suddenly and the thin gold light is obliterated. In winter the common cycle of weather as indicated by the cloud formations goes awry. Most of the year one can roughly gauge the storm cycles by the cumulus, cirrus, stratus, and nimbus clouds, which follow each other in that sequence. In December, January, and February along the sea it seems as though the stratus clouds hang low for days and then change to nimbus. It is this latter type that spews sleet, snow, and driving rain.

158

If one makes repeated trips to the same spot, he can feel the increasing pressure of the wind as the barometer steadily drops. Gone is the steady, rhythmic roll of the waves. The waters begin to feel the power of the wind. Angrily the rollers break, and the choppy waves shoulder one another into pieces. When the water flattens on the sands of the beach, there's a loud, sullen hissing as the thinning sheets curl and writhe and twist back toward the ocean. Like 10,000 vindictive serpents, they coil and flow, unite and separate, stretch and contract. And when the receding waters meet the brutal strength of the oncoming waves, there is a battle between the forces of gravity and the pulsating might of the ocean.

One can feel the marshaling power of the storm. Gusts of cold wind with winter-keen edges whip pieces of flotsam, grass, and seaweed into the air. A breath of the storm with sudden fury takes a wave high onto the beach. Arrows of cold sleet and rain begin to slant through the air. Ripples of motion run across the marshes as the frost-killed grasses bend before the wind. On the drumlins the scrubby oaks, sumacs, and gray birches begin to whip back and forth.

Minute by minute one can feel the force of the storm increase. The rain and sleet change to particles of hard snow. Even at midday one can see only a few feet around him on the beach. The wind moans and shrieks in the dunes behind; the sea is a mass of ugly, powerful waves ridden by a snarling band of dragons. The pounding of the waves is like the blows of Vulcan's hammer; it's like the climax of a great soul-stirring symphony after a seemingly interminable build-up by brasses and drums. To keep one's feet in the face of the gale, it is necessary to lean far forward into the wind. It is merciless, heartless, impersonal.

The gods hurl their heaviest legions at the land. Great ice packs form on the marshes; the water undercuts banks and beaches. Never again in all eternity will that stretch of coast line be just as it was before. A man can take only so much of the bitterness; soon he has to leave the lonely, tortured beach to suffer through the storm.

Ewing Galloway, New York

Ocean's Mystery

❖ ❖

SINCE THE BEGINNING of history, man has acknowledged the mystery of the great waters. No one knows when the first human being stood on a beach, headland, or mountain and looked in wide-eyed wonder at the seemingly limitless expanse. Long before man began to make written symbols to record his thoughts and deeds, he learned to make rafts and dugouts and to travel along the edge of the ocean. Because of the mighty power and awesome loneliness of the vast stretches, he invented legends and evolved superstitions about the ocean.

It took thousands of years for man to discover the truth about the seas and their relationship to the lands we call continents. Today great ships plow through the water; man-made contraptions go beneath it; and the air-borne ships envisioned by Leonardo da Vinci travel high above it. Man has conquered space but not the ocean. The Gargantuan valleys that hold our seas between continents are a law unto themselves. Twice in each day the attraction of the sun and moon sends legions of water surging against the land; twice in each day the sea calls its forces back. In spring and fall, periods of the great tides, when a northeast storm coincides with the full of the moon, there's an epochal assault, and the angry waters cut new patterns in the dunes and beaches.

Probably in due time the mysteries of the sea will be solved— the migrations of the fishes, the myriad forms of ancient life at the bottom of the ocean. Meanwhile, the men who go down to the sea for its uncertain harvest, those who travel on it or above it, and the many human beings who go to its shores for recreation and for restoration of strength know that a part of the charm of the great waters is the age-old sense of mystery that broods over its eternally restless surface.

A Note about the Sea-food Recipes That Follow

✿ ✿

FOOD AND GOOD FELLOWSHIP have long been the Damon and Pythias of mankind's social life. Most persons have discovered that, when other topics of conversation fail, food is a common bond of interest.

In *The Countryman's Cookbook* appeared the following assertion: "One doesn't have to be a learned philosopher to know that peace and security for the nations of the world will never be realized until all men and women, boys and girls, and little children everywhere have enough to eat. If I were making the world over, the first thing I would do would be to make sure all human beings get enough to eat."

Food is important, even though these essays are written in a light vein. The recipe of writing that has been followed in them is a combination of whimsey and lightness, shaded with seasonings of truth and time-tested facts that will enable the reader to enjoy preparing the dishes. A part of the flavor of the sea, surely, is the enjoyment of the good food that is harvested from it. There may be differences of opinion on the ways to prepare some of the dishes; but it can be agreed that foods from the ocean have an important place in everybody's life.

163

Clam Chowder

✿ ✿

IT IS DOUBTFUL that the rumor is true that Jupiter called first for a bowl of clam chowder and failing to get it settled for a plate of ambrosia. Jupiter would not compromise to that extent. It is hardly credible that some people put stewed tomatoes into clam chowder; it's heresy of the first order to know that some urbanites not only use tomatoes but also toss in odds and ends of any vegetables available.

A genuine clam chowder is made in just one way. There's no point in arguing; no international conferences can sway the opinions of those who have been on speaking terms with edible bivalves since their third or fourth birthdays. The real thing is made with a quart or two of clams, a few potatoes, plenty of dried-out salt pork, onions, whole milk, pepper, salt, and butter.

The whole is harmoniously fused together in a slow, flavor-blending process. The goal is the inseparable union of the various ingredients into one nostril-tickling concoction. There are those who spurn the golden-brown rivulets of fat from the salt pork. This is probably the same group that uses white corn meal for johnnycake. But a bowl of hot, steaming clam chowder without the browned salt pork and its liquid is like apple pie without cinnamon.

After the chowder is made, it must cool awhile and then be reheated just before eating. Naturally, the liquid is thickened with flour. It has been reported that there are individuals who do neither, but that is simply middle-of-the-twentieth-century propaganda. Clam chowder, to be authentic, is served with a pat of butter spreading over the top and with four halves of Boston common crackers thoroughly soaked. When a man has had about a quart of this, he's fortified for a spell of work.

Fried Lobster

✿ ✿

ACCORDING TO a news item, freight-carrying airplanes will soon be delivering live lobsters to all sections of the nation. That's an excellent idea. More unification will result if all citizens learn to use lobster occasionally. Unfortunately, this marine crustacean has been a luxury item up to now. However, the Federal and State governments are beginning to interest themselves in scientific propagation of the prehistoric-looking creature, and it may be that soon a feasible method of insuring a sufficient supply will be evolved.

One hesitates to be dogmatic in a kaleidoscopic world, but next to lobster stew, fried lobster comes first. Altogether too few citizens, even in lobster-yielding territory, know the secrets of making first-flight fried lobster. To begin with, there must be enough so a man feels that he's had a feed. It is better to have it less often than to tantalize oneself with an insufficiency. For each person there should be at least 10 ounces of meat.

The meat should come from boiled live lobsters and should be thoroughly chilled before it's fried. Don't listen to any nonsense about frying it as soon as it's mined from the critter. Put it in the icebox overnight. Then the next day it's aged enough so that the complete flavor can be brought out. Cut it in chunks the size of pullets' eggs. Put lots of butter in an old-fashioned iron spider over a wood fire. Then toss the pieces in. Keep a cover over the spider for 5 minutes. From time to time stir the pieces around. Fried lobster needs heat, but not too much. By and by, when little flecks of brown come on the outside and the meat is piping hot all the way through, it's ready. Pour the butter gravy on a slice of well-browned toast and heap the fried lobster on it. Eating the fragrant, rich, satisfying goodness of it is enjoying one of the best crops harvested from the ocean.

Fried Clams

✿ ✿

THE DICTIONARY dismisses the clam with its usual terse and impersonal comment. The leading statement is, "Any of various bivalve mollusks." It adds a little to know that the clam has a siphon and incurrent and excurrent orifices. Most persons know it has a shell; some know it has a foot. Most citizens think of it in terms of clam chowder, scalloped clams, or fried clams. To them, all clam *materia,* like Gaul, is divided into three parts. And from the smell along Route 1, all the way from Florida to the Canadian line, fried clams are first in popularity.

A man likes fried clams. There's something about the chewy, nutty, tangy goodness of them that appeals. There's no other food quite like them. But there are fried clams and fried clams. A few places know how to prepare and cook them correctly, and they richly deserve the patronage they receive. Naturally, the main ingredients are first-quality freshly dug clams. Other than that there are two main secrets of superb fried clams. First, the batter must be made of exactly the right proportions: 1¼ cups of general-purpose flour, ⅔ teaspoon of salt, a scant ¾ cup of rich milk, a whiffet of pepper, and 2 beaten eggs. A little more or less flour or more or less milk may be needed. It takes experience to judge when the batter is just right—neither too moist nor too dry. And the milk must be rich and creamy. There are some who scoff, but if 1 tablespoon of melted butter and a bit of sugar are added to the batter, the added flavor will be a happy surprise. When it comes to frying the clams, there's only one secret: the fat must be hot, a bit above 375 degrees.

Clams are a plain, plebeian dish, and it's best to eat them with one's fingers. No one knows what pioneer housewife made the first batter and fried her family a mess of the bivalve mollusks. But fried clams have played their role as a good food ever since man sought a part of his sustenance from the sea.

166

Codfish Cakes

✿ ✿

SOMETIMES A MAN likes to think a bit on how everyday items of food have helped shape the world's history. There's reason to believe that long before Columbus started across the Atlantic with the *Niña,* the *Pinta,* and the *Santa Maria* the Vikings and Basques knew of the great schools of codfish along the banks of Newfoundland. There are claims that the English visited the fishing grounds near Iceland as early as 1415. The cod was important enough in our nation's early history to be placed upon the colonial seal of Massachusetts, and at one time it was on a Nova Scotian bank note with the cheering legend, "Success to the Fisheries."

As a matter of information, one is glad to know that the largest cod ever taken in New England waters weighed 211½ pounds. But what interests the shoreman most is the best way or ways to use *Gadus callarias linneaus.* Fish chowder, scalloped fish with cheese sauce, baked cod with plenty of dressing are all good. But day in and day out, especially for breakfast, nothing quite has the zip and zest of correctly made and fried codfish cakes.

Basically they're a simple food: 1½ cups of cold, boiled shredded fish, 1 generous cup of cold mashed potatoes, 2 beaten eggs, a little diced onion, just a smidgen of mustard, and a dite of celery salt. The secrets of first-rate codfish cakes are two: first, the ingredients must be well mixed the night before and allowed to blend their flavors overnight into one harmonious whole; second, they must be fried slowly in lots of butter. After they are heated through, increase the heat and get a thick, golden-brown crunchy crust on both sides. If a man has three or four of these, plus other staples and a piece of juicy deep-dish apple pie for a topper-off, he has a breakfast that sticks to his ribs for the forenoon's work.

Oyster Stew

✿ ✿

THIS MARINE BIVALVE MOLLUSK is excellent eating in many ways. Men who are discriminating and whose judgments are valid say that for flavor and deliciousness scalloped oysters head the list. But those who pronounce this verdict on Ostreidae are quick to add that oyster stew has a secure niche of its own in the hall of food fame. The man who first broke apart the shells of this bivalve, cooked the mussel, and then ate it, deserves to have his courage sung in the company of heroes. He brought to mankind's notice a food and flavor that many enjoy.

Sophisticated city dwellers must realize that an oyster stew is not a chowder. One deplores the admission that some people actually use potatoes with oysters. Boston oyster chowder has a degree of local fame, but it's nothing that compares in the same breath with baked beans or codfish. The genuine, original, full-flavored oyster stew is compounded of 1 quart of oysters, 1 quart of very rich milk, 2 heaped tablespoons of butter, a smidgen of onion salt, and regular salt and pepper. Don't try to gild the lily by adding parsley, strips of onion, or any other floral or faunal matters.

Put the strained oyster liquor in a saucepan and heat it to just below the boiling point. Warm the milk in a double boiler. When it's piping hot but not boiling, add the oyster liquor. Next, put in onion salt, salt, and pepper. A minute or two after the liquid is seasoned, stir in the oysters. When the oysters puff up and are well crinkled at the edges, they are done. Use will power! Set the dish on the back of the stove to cool. It's the reheating at suppertime that brings out that nose-twitching, saliva-starting, air-filling aroma that denotes the perfect oyster stew.

Scalloped Fish

* *

JUST BECAUSE so few know the gustatory satisfaction of scalloped fish is no reason why a man shouldn't do a little missionary work and proclaim its virtues to the world. It has taken time for many delectable and nutritious foods to overcome unfounded prejudices and unintelligent mental attitudes. Tomatoes were called "poison apples" once upon a time. No doubt the man who first boiled and ate a clam deserves mention in the book of heroes. The shoreman feels a sense of pitying impatience for those who only use fish when it's fried or in chowder.

Scalloped fish is an easy dish to prepare, but it requires will power to wait for it to ripen to its peak of perfection. As with beef stew and clam chowder, it should never be eaten the day it is assembled and cooked. That uplifting experience should come on the second or third day. Basically, the dish is a mixture of flaked cooked fish, a white milk sauce made very rich with plenty of cream and butter, a few fried mushrooms, and a whiffet of fried onion—just enough to impart that delicate, tangy, mouth-watering flavor that only onion can give to a dish.

Use plenty of fish, and be sure to mix in a few small pieces of sharp cheese. Put a good layer of butter over the bottom of the baking dish. Fill the dish ⅔ full of fish, and pour over the sauce, the mushrooms, and the onions. Poke the cheese bits down into the innards. Spread a cupful or so of bread crumbs over the top, and bake in a hot oven. The person with will power will put the cooked dish in the refrigerator overnight. The person without will power will eat some for supper and will save the rest for the next day. Scalloped fish is just a trifle heavy for breakfast, but from lunch time on until the bedtime snack, it is a food that gives a man something to work on.

Cream of Clam Soup

✿ ✿

NATURALLY ENOUGH, perhaps, clams have had their praises sung as the foundation of chowder. A few discerning people know the deep satisfaction of scalloped clams. Fried clams are standard equipment; all along the sea's edge in summer one can smell them as they are sold from the shanties and stores that make Route 1 from Florida to Maine the greatest restaurant road in the world. But only a handful of people know the deliciousness of cream of clam soup. In a harried, edgy world a person is entitled to ponder the business of living. Anyone who tries to be philosophical regarding mankind's foibles knows that clam soup will remain important long after contemporary festerings have faded to insignificance.

Like most really superlative foods, it's a simple dish: 1 quart of drained clams, 1 quart of very rich milk, salt to taste, a whisker of pepper, 3 level tablespoons of flour (more or less), and 3 generous tablespoons of butter. Use the juice of the drained clams and a little water in which to simmer the heads of the clams for 10 or 15 minutes. Mix the flour and some of the milk, and cook for 4 or 5 minutes, stirring all the time. Have the rest of the milk heating very, very slowly in a double boiler. Then add the flour mixture, the liquid from the simmered hard parts, the chopped soft parts of the clams, the salt, and the pepper. Cook 5 minutes more, and add the butter. Now—and this is one of the major secrets—set the soup aside to cool. The reheating brings out that superlative, tantalizing fragrance that foretells the smooth, creamy deliciousness of the dish.

Lobster Newburg

✿ ✿

ONE HESITATES to be dogmatic about foods, especially where this macrural crustacean is concerned. The adherents of boiled lobster are staunch and articulate; the school that favors lobster salad is not noted for its reticence; the group that votes for lobster stew is granite firm in its convictions. Perhaps it is best to say simply, in regard to Newburg, that there is only one way to prepare this dish so that the full, fragrant, tantalizing aroma fills the kitchen and gives happy promise of the feast to come.

For the benefit of all, a few fundamental ordinances must be laid down. Newburg cannot be made with milk; it is not a dish one stirs up and then forgets as it cooks. The cook must give it his (or her) concentrated attention. Heat 1¾ cups of light cream in a double boiler; then pour it over 2 beaten egg yolks. Stir and replace in boiler and cook a few minutes, stirring all the time. When this mixture is thickened, add 3½ cups of chopped lobster meat. Cook for 6 minutes and 35$\frac{7}{10}$ seconds. Then stir in a piece of butter the size of a year-old baby's fist.

That's lobster Newburg—rich, tasty, chewy, and satisfying. There are many who prefer it served on well-buttered toast; a few know the goodness of it on fluffy, creamy mashed potatoes. But some men who have experimented, men who are not necessarily fussy but simply discriminating, say that to enjoy the ultimate flavor of this dish of the sea one should open two brown-crusted, freshly baked homemade biscuits, put the four halves in the bottom of a big soup plate, butter the biscuits generously, and then pour on a heaping cupful of the mixture.

Fish Hash

✿ ✿

ON A COOLISH DAY in late spring or early summer, when a man has been working through the afternoon at a seasonal task, there's a degree of comfort in knowing that suppertime is likely to mean fish hash. Too few members of the race labeled *Homo sapiens* know the satisfying, chewy goodness of it. Fish in many forms is good eating; boiled, fried, baked, or broiled, the various kinds have their staunch protagonists.

Fish hash has never really come into its own. One readily admits it's a plebeian, everyday sort of mixture, and doubtless many a housewife thinks of it in the same category with carelessly tossed together potatoes and meat. However, the shoreman whose helpmeet really knows the art of blending a superb hash is contented when he sees plenty of fish left over from dinner. The midday meal is important, but the prospect of a favorite supper helps a man through the hours after high twelve.

There are secrets to making a fish hash. In the first place, the proportions among the ingredients need to be reasonably accurate. Careful experimentation, due deliberation, and sober cogitation lead one to say that perfect amalgamation comes from 60 per cent cold mashed potatoes, 30 per cent shredded boned fish, 5 per cent onion, and 5 per cent crisp pieces of fried salt pork. The ingredients should be chopped in a big wooden bowl until well blended and then fried in an old-fashioned iron spider in a generous amount of butter. Pat the mixture down firmly. Fry it until the bottom is a thick, brown crunchy crust. Serve with plenty of sweet cucumber pickles. Two helpings of this, a couple of wedges of molasses pie, and a glass of milk make one of the good ways to end a day's labor.

Cape Cod Quahog Cakes

✿ ✿

AN IMPATIENT, temperamental sort of person had better leave clam cakes alone. If he likes to prepare something and to eat it immediately, he will have to add clam cakes to lobster stew and clam chowder as something to pass by. Certain food combinations have to mellow a bit before the trial by fire. The ingredients need time to get acquainted and blend into each other's qualities. On the other hand, if a person is forehanded and likes to prepare supper in the early part of the day, here is an excellent dish that can be made after breakfast and cooked in a few minutes before mealtime.

Experiment a little to get a batter of just the right degree of consistency. Mix the batter of egg, flour, and rich milk. Use a cupful or so of bread crumbs. The foundation is 1½ quarts of quahog meats and the juice of the quahogs. Grind up the quahogs and before stirring them into the batter add a bit of ground onion. (A piece of onion the size of a ten-year-old's thumb end is about right.)

The mixture should sit in peaceful relaxation for at least 8 hours. Then, at suppertime, mold into cakes lightly pressed into shape and fry in a hot, old-fashioned iron spider on the front hole of a wood-burning stove. The best fuel is a combination of white birch and rock maple. Anyone who is unfortunate enough to live in a modern house *can* achieve satisfying cakes in an aluminum frying pan over electricity or gas. Six or eight good-sized crunchy cakes, a few cream-of-tartar, brown-crusted biscuits, some wild-grape jelly, a cereal dish of Indian pudding, and a glass or two of cold creamy milk comprise a very acceptable meal.

Fish Chowder

✿ ✿

STRANGELY ENOUGH, there are otherwise intelligent persons who disdain fish chowder. The gentleman who wrote a best seller by the simple expedient of putting one word after another in alphabetical order did not bother to go into details. He admitted that clams or fish mixed with milk, potatoes, and onions constituted a dish called chowder. That will pass as a safe generalization, but it is far from satisfactory to those who know the piquant, nostril-tickling, saliva-starting qualities of fish chowder when it is made correctly.

First of all, it must be prepared in an old iron kettle, and second, it must be cooked on a wood-burning kitchen stove. Modern efficiency, as exemplified by gas and electricity, is all right for some things but not for fish chowder. A good many dishes can only attain superlative heights of gastronomical deliciousness when cooked over well-seasoned maple, oak, birch, or hickory.

First, try out several slices of salt pork in an iron spider. Make sure the pork has some meat in it, for the tangy bits of meat add an essential edge to the flavor. When the pork is crusty brown, cut it into very small cubes. Place the cubes and 60 per cent of the fat in the bottom of the iron kettle sitting on a hole cover over a slow fire. Put in 3 quarts of whole milk and 1 cupful of cream. Cut up 3 onions the sizes of eggs. Much onion is essential. Now add 6 cut-up, half-cooked potatoes and 2 pounds of boned and cooked fish.

This is the foundation. Let the mixture heat very slowly; never let it boil. Keep the fire moderate. When the chowder is piping hot and sending forth waves of delicious aroma, move it to the back of the stove to cool slowly for 2 hours. Then set it out on the porch to chill. This is why it's important to make fish chowder in the forenoon. About 4 o'clock in the afternoon put it back on the stove and reheat until it's piping hot. That's how one gets the full flavor of fish chowder.

174

Scalloped Oysters

✧ ✧

IT's ODD how names get attached to foods. When a person says "scalloped" oysters, he refers to "the valves of a scallop shell or a similarly shaped dish, used for baking." That's what Mr. Webster says. He departs enough from his customary taciturnity to remark, "To bake in a scallop casserole, etc., as oysters or tomatoes prepared with bread crumbs or other ingredients." It's interesting that Noah mentions oysters and tomatoes. Both are delicious, but there is no question in a shoreman's mind about the relative merits of the two. On a cold fall or winter night a big dish of scalloped oysters is as close to gustatory heaven as one will get on this planet.

There are a few pointers that must be observed if the dish is to be eaten at its superlative best. The casual airiness of contemporary culinary procedures does not jibe with the preparation of this food. The basic ingredients are 1 quart of fresh-shucked oysters, 1 cup of cream, 2 cups of moist bread crumbs, ⅔ cup of melted butter, 1 teaspoon of celery salt, and salt and pepper. Butter the casserole generously and fill it up with alternating layers of oysters and crumbs, adding salt and pepper along the way. Pour on the cream and melted butter; sprinkle on a little celery salt. Cover with more crumbs and bake about 45 minutes in a 400-degree oven.

Those are the instructions; they are needed as guideposts. But a man who is particular, though not necessarily fussy, realizes that sometimes it takes just a mite more or less of cream to get the right consistency. And no one, unless driven by some mysterious barbaric instinct, would think of using cracker crumbs.

At the end of a day's work spent in battening down boats for the winter or overhauling lobster pots in the old shanty on the pier, a man is grateful for a generous helping of this fragrant, moist goodness. Scalloped oysters do not make a dish with flossy airs but they do make a man feel that most of the world's limitations are due to his own short circuits.

175

Clam Pie

✿ ✿

ONE CAN PRESENT substantial evidence in favor of making a whole meal from any of many different kinds of pies. Some happy day when human beings are civilized sufficiently to dispense with such contemporary essentials as bubble gum and overly enthusiastic radio announcers, they will have sufficient perspicacity to eat their desserts at the proper time. There are many signs of unthinking subservience to tradition but few with such unhappy results as the timeworn idea that dessert should be eaten after a sufficiency of food. If persons ate desserts first, when taste buds are keenest, not only would they more fully enjoy the taste, but also they would not be so easily tempted to overeat.

Clam pie, however, is not a dessert. It is a main dish and as far as the shoreman is concerned, it can be the only dish at a meal. It is a simple dish to concoct if one abides by a few fundamentals. Use a pie plate at least $1\frac{15}{16}$ inches deep. Line it with a first-rate pastry crust. No hand that is inclined to skimp should ever make piecrust for any type of pie. Grind up the necks and chop up the stomachs of the clams. Cook them for 8 or 10 minutes in water with a few pieces of amenable onions. Thicken the broth with a smidgen of flour. Then put the mixture in the pie plate and tuck on the upper crust. Bake at 350 degrees for about 15 or 20 minutes. Don't try to pin things down to dogmatic details; good cooks like a little leeway. That's all there is to clam pie. But when it comes from the oven, piping hot, fragrant, and nostril-satisfying, its fragrance steals out to the woodshed. As a man comes in from his day's work and whiffs that aroma, he is content with his day of living.

Lobster Stew

❋ ❋

ONCE IN A WHILE instead of tersely defining a given subject, one wishes that Mr. Webster had used an adjective that expressed some degree of enthusiasm. This is especially the case in regard to certain edible materials. About lobsters, the book of words merely states, "Any large marine macrural crustacean used as food, esp. those of a genus (*Homarus*) with stalked compound eyes, and five pairs of legs, of which the first two are modified into enormous chelae, or pincers."

It is difficult to understand why no mention is made of lobster stew as the best way to use this crustacean for food. There are some who mistakenly press for boiled lobster, lobster Newburg, and lobster thermidor. But one expects such diversions and alarms. There are even those who talk enthusiastically about lobster salad. However, the fundamental and basic use of the delicious, bland, chewy meat should be in lobster stew.

There's an art in compounding the mixture, simple though it is in basic construction. The basic ingredients are about 2 pounds of the meat, which includes the tomalley, or liver, and the thick white substance inside the shell. Simmer the latter two together for 10 minutes in a generous ½ cup of butter; add the cut-up lobster meat; cook 10 minutes more. Push the kettle to the back of the stove, and when the mixture has cooled about 25½ degrees, very, very slowly add 1½ quarts of rich creamy milk and 1 pint of light cream. Stirring in the milk and cream is one of the major points of a perfect lobster stew. The second major point is to let the stew cool for a full day before reheating for serving. When the time comes to put it on for supper, heat slowly and add a bit of salt and pepper and plenty of butter.

Scalloped Clams

✿ ✿

THE DIVERGENCE of opinion regarding the common thick-shelled round, or hard, clam or quahog (*Venus mercenaria*), and the common thin-shelled long, or soft, clam having long siphons (*Mya arenaria*) comes to the fore when solid citizens with long experience debate the best ways of using the edible bivalve mollusks. One admits that the adherents of each school have much weighty evidence. There's something about clam chowder, for example—that is, the New England concoction. In foreign parts, like New York City, tomatoes, green peppers, carrots, and no one knows what other dreadful ingredients are used. Then there's one hardy clan that holds out for fried clams; and still another vociferous minority that stands adamant for clam fritters.

The shoreman, who uses both the ocean and the land for his livelihood, claims that nothing quite equals scalloped clams. He uses 1 quart of shucked clams and chops up the necks and heads. Then he mixes these and the soft portions with 1 pint of rich milk, about 3 cups of bread crumbs, 2 beaten eggs, a generous ½ cup of butter, salt and pepper, and a diced onion. He stirs the whole dishful well and bakes it for about 45 minutes in a moderate oven. When it comes to the table, steaming hot, fragrant, brown, and crusted, he knows he has a supper that utilizes correctly the edible bivalve mollusks. Topped off with a piece of spicy rhubarb pie and a glass of cold, creamy milk, it's a good way to end a day's hoeing in the cornfield.